EDITORIAL

Big Brother at the border

Travel restrictions and snooping into your social media at the frontier are new ways of suppressing ideas, says **Rachael Jolley**

48(03): 01/03 I DOI: 10.1177/0306422019876483

TRAVELLING TO THE USA this summer, journalist James Dyer, who writes for Empire magazine, says he was not allowed in until he had been questioned by an immigration official about whether he wrote for those "fake news" outlets.

Also this year, David Mack, deputy director of breaking news at Buzzfeed News, was challenged about the way his organisation covered a story at the US border by an official. He later received an official apology from the Customs and Border Protection service for being questioned on this subject, which is not on the official list of queries that officers are expected to use.

As we go to press, the UK Foreign Office updated its advice for travellers going between Hong Kong and China warning that their electronic devices could be searched. This happened a day after a Sky journalist had his

belongings, including photos, searched at Beijing airport.

US citizen Hugo Castro (see p26) told Index how he was held for five hours at the USA-Mexico border while his mobile phone, photos and social media were searched.

This kind of behaviour is becoming more widespread globally as nations look to surveil what thoughts we have and what we might be writing or saying before allowing us to pass.

This ends with many people being so worried about the consequences of putting pen to paper that they don't.

They fret so much about being prevented from travelling to see a loved one or a friend, or going on a work trip, that they stop themselves from writing or expressing dissent.

If the world spins further in this direction we will end up with a global climate of fear where we second-guess our desire to write, tweet, speak or protest, by worrying ourselves down a timeline of what might happen next.

So what is the situation today? Border officials in some countries already seek to find out about your sexual orientation via an excursion into your social media presence as part of their decision on whether to allow you in.

Travel advisors who offer LGBT travel advice suggest not giving up your passcodes or passwords to social media accounts. One says that, before travelling, people can look at hiding their social media posts from people they might stay with in the destination country. Digital security expert Ela Stapley suggests going further and having an entirely separate "clean" phone for travelling (see p32). →

EDITOR-IN-CHIEF
Rachael Jolley
DEPUTY EDITOR
Sally Gimson
SUB EDITORS
Tracey Bagshaw,
Adam Aiken

CONTRIBUTING EDITORS
Irene Caselli, Jan Fox
(USA),
Kaya Genç (Turkey),
Laura Silvia Battaglia
(Yemen and Iraq),
Stephen Woodman
(Mexico)

EDITORIAL ASSISTANT
Lewis Jennings
ART DIRECTOR
Matthew Hasteley
COVER
Ben Jennings

THANKS TO
Sean Gallagher,
Ryan McChrystal

MAGAZINE PRINTED BY
Page Bros.,
Norwich UK

INDEX ON CENSORSHIP
indexcensorship.org I +44 (0) 20 3848 9820 I 1 Rivington Place, London EC2A 3BA, United Kingdom

Supported by
**ARTS COUNCIL
ENGLAND**

can to help it compile a personal profile of everyone who uses it. There's no doubt that if companies are doing this, governments are thinking about how they can do it too – if they are not already. And the more they know, the more they can work out what they want to stop.

In democracies such as the UK, police are already experimenting with facial recognition software. Recently, anti-surveillance organisation Big Brother Watch discovered that private shopping centres had quietly started to use facial recognition software without the public being aware. It feels as though everywhere we look, everyone is capturing more and more information about who we are, and we need to worry about how this is being used.

One way that this information can be used is by border officials, who would like to know everything about you as they consider your arrival. What we've learned in putting this special issue together is that we need to be smart, too. Keep an eye on the laws of the country you are travelling to, in case legislation relating to media, communication or even visas change. Also, have a plan about what you might do if you are stopped at a border.

One of the big themes of this magazine over the years is that what happens in one country doesn't stay in one country. What has become increasingly obvious is that nation copies nation, and leader after leader spots what is going on across the way and thinks: "I could use that too."

We saw troll factories start in Mexico with attempts to discredit journalists' reputations five years ago, and now they are widespread. The idea of a national leader speaking directly to the public rather than giving a press conference, and skipping the "need" to answer questions, was popular in Latin America with President Cristina Fernández de Kirchner , of Argentina, and Venezuelan President Hugo Chávez. A few years later, national leaders around the world have grabbed the idea and

→   These actions at borders have not gone unnoticed by technology providers. The big dating apps are aware that information to be found in their spaces might also prove of interest to immigration officials in some countries. This summer, Tinder rolled out a feature called Traveller Alert – as Mark Frary reports on p23 – which hides people's profiles if they are travelling to countries where homosexuality is illegal.

Borders are getting bigger, harder and tougher. It is not just about people travelling, it's also about knowledge and ideas being stopped. As security services and governments get more tech-savvy, they see more and more ways to keep track of the words that we share. Surely there's no one left out there who doesn't realise the messages in their Gmail account are constantly being scanned and collected by Google as the quid pro quo for giving you a free account? Google is collecting as much information as it

CREDIT: Gary Waters/Ikon

run with it. It's so we don't have to filter it through the media, say the politicians. While there's nothing wrong, of course, with having town hall chats with the public, one has a sneaking suspicion that another motivation might be dodging any difficult questions, especially if press conferences then get put on hold. Again, Latin America saw it first.

Given this trend, we can expect that when one nation starts asking for access to your social media accounts before they give you a visa, others are sure to follow.

The border issue is broader than this, of course. Migration and immigration are issues all over the world right now, topping most political agendas, along with security and the economy. Therefore, governments are seeking to reduce immigration and restrict who can enter their countries – using a variety of methods.

In the USA and the UK, artists, academics, writers and musicians are finding visas harder to come by. As our US contributing editor, Jan Fox, reports, this has led to an opera singer removing posts from Facebook because she worries about her visa application, and academics self-censoring their ideas in case it limits them from studying or working in the USA (see page 16).

Where does this leave free expression? Less free than it should be, certainly.

This is not the only attack on freedom of expression. Making it more difficult for outsiders to travel to these countries means stories about life in Yemen, Syria and Iran, for instance, may not be heard.

We don't hear firsthand what it is like, and our knowledge shrinks. This policy surely reached a limit when Kareem Abeed, the Syrian producer of an Oscar-nominated documentary about Aleppo, was initially refused a visa to attend the Oscar ceremony (see p16). Meanwhile, UK festival directors are calling for their government to change its attitude and warn that artists are already excluding the UK from their tours.

One person who knew the value of getting information out beyond the borders of the country he lived in was a former editor of this magazine, Andrew Graham-Yooll, and we honour his work in this issue. His recent death

> *We can expect that when one nation starts asking for access to your social media accounts before giving you a visa, others are sure to follow*

gave us a chance to review his writing for us and for others. A consummate journalist, Graham-Yooll continued to write and report until just weeks before his death, and I know he would have had his typing fingers at the ready for a critique of what is happening in the Argentinian election right now.

Graham-Yooll took the job of editor of Index on Censorship in 1989, after being forced to leave his native Argentina because of his reporting. He had been smuggling out reports of the horrifying things that were happening under the dictatorship, where people who were activists, journalists and critics of the government were "disappearing" – a soft word that means they were being murdered. Some pregnant women were taken prisoner until they gave birth. Their babies were taken from them and given to military or government-friendly families to adopt, while the mothers were drugged and then dropped to their death, from airplanes, at sea.

Many of the appalling details of what happened under the authoritarian dictatorship only became clear after it fell, but Graham-Yooll took measures to smuggle out as many details as he could, to this publication and others, until he and his family were in such danger he was forced to leave Argentina and move to the UK (see page 68).

Throughout history the powerful have always attempted to suppress information they didn't want to see the light. We are in yet another era where this is on the rise. ⊗

Rachael Jolley is editor-in-chief of Index on Censorship

CONTENTS

VOLUME 48 NUMBER 03 – AUTUMN 2019

CREDIT: Ben Jennings

IN FOCUS

CULTURE

CHIEF EXECUTIVE
Jodie Ginsberg

EDITOR-IN-CHIEF
Rachael Jolley

HEAD OF CONTENT
Sean Gallagher

FINANCE DIRECTOR
David Sewell

HEAD OF ADVOCACY
Joy Hyvarinen

HEAD OF OPERATIONS
Matt Townsend

DEPUTY EDITOR
Sally Gimson

ASSISTANT EDITOR, ONLINE AND NEWS
Ryan McChrystal

EVENTS AND PARTNERSHIPS PRODUCER
Helen Galliano

FELLOWSHIPS OFFICER
Perla Hinojosa

ADVOCACY OFFICER
Jessica Ní Mhainín

EDITORIAL ASSISTANT
Lewis Jennings

OFFICE MANAGER
Rosie Gilbey

ASSOCIATE PRODUCER
Julia Farrington

DIRECTORS & TRUSTEES
Trevor Phillips (Chair), David Aaronovitch, Anthony Barling, Kate Maltby, Sanjay Nazerali, Elaine Potter, David Schlesinger, Mark Stephens, Kiri Kankhwende

PATRONS
Margaret Atwood, Simon Callow, Steve Coogan, Brian Eno, Harold Evans, Christopher Hird, Lord Joel Joffe, Jude Kelly, Michael Palin, Matthew Parris, Alexandra Pringle, Gabrielle Rifkind, Sir Tom Stoppard, Lady Sue Woodford Hollick

ADVISORY COMMITTEE
Julian Baggini, Clemency Burton-Hill, Ariel Dorfman, Michael Foley, Andrew Franklin, Conor Gearty, AC Grayling, Lyndsay Griffiths, William Horsley, Anthony Hudson, Natalia Koliada, Jane Kramer, Htein Lin, Jean-Paul Marthoz, Robert McCrum, Rebecca MacKinnon, Beatrice Mtetwa,

Julian Petley, Michael Scammell, Kamila Shamsie, Michael Smyth, Tess Woodcraft, Christie Watson

X
48.03

PICTURED: A border patrol officer stands guard at a 30-foot border wall in the El Centro Sector, at the US/Mexico border in Calexico, California on 26 October 2018

CREDIT: Mark Ralston/AFP

SPECIAL REPORT

BORDER FORCES
How Barriers To Free Thought Got Tough

Switch off, we're landing!

Travellers to Turkey should be prepared for what they are not allowed to do or read. **Kaya Genç** reports on what is out of bounds

48(03): 08/10 | DOI: 10.1177/0306422019876434

WHEN FOREIGN VISITORS land in Turkey and pass border control, some things are taken from them – and they might not see it coming. They can no longer access Wikipedia. They can't scroll through social media accounts banned by the Turkish government. They can't log on to "pornography".

Unlike North Korea, Turkey doesn't yet have its own intranet with sites disconnected from the world. Instead, the Turkish internet is a slightly redacted version of the original.

Over the past decade, as part of a nationalistic drive, Turkey has more keenly defended its borders to control information coming in and out of the country. As a result, censorship is taking subtle new forms. Since the early 2010s, as the country has become politically more isolated and has turned its back on its EU accession goals, Turkish control over the flow of information slowly increased. Once considered a bridge between East and West, Turkey began to resemble a border between continents.

Placing physical borders on the flow of information, in a nation of 82 million people, is a Herculean task demanding immense budgets and dedicated personnel. Turkey has recently focused its energies on two fronts. First, authorities use digital borders to control information coming into the country. Secondly, they use physical borders to control reporters and visitors who travel in and out.

This task was outsourced to the Information and Communication Technologies Authority. Founded in 2000, the ICTA oversees a budget of more than $900 million and employs a staff of about 640.

Seven years earlier, the internet had arrived. It came on 12 April 1993 via routers installed inside the Middle Eastern Technical University in Ankara, posing a challenge to the authorities' grip on information. The early 1990s, a catastrophic time for human rights, had seen torture becoming rampant in police stations; prosecutors eagerly pursuing prison sentences for dissidents; and Kurdish political activists routinely suffering forced disappearances. By the time the first internet access provider was founded in 1996, dissidents hoped the internet might loosen Turkey's political borders.

In 2001, about the time Western magazines were hailing Turkey as a bridge between East and West, the Turkish parliament passed a law to regulate the internet. Numerous websites, mostly those related to Kurdish separatist groups and the hard left, became inaccessible. After 2005, the pace of bans accelerated. In 2007, Turkey shut off access to YouTube after it failed to remove a video about Turkey's founder, Mustafa Kemal Atatürk. The same year, a Muslim evangelist preacher named Adnan Oktar used a Turkish court order to shut down the blogging website WordPress, not just the page about him, but all WordPress-hosted sites, which disappeared overnight.

The legal framework for such border control actions is murky. In 2011, the ruling AKP (Justice and Development Party) passed a law to create the "safe" use of the internet; three years later, it gave the ICTA the right to shut down websites it didn't like within four hours.

As the government became more inward-looking politically, its border patrols on information grew. In 2014, the ICTA closed Twitter for a time, using a law that made it possible based on "privacy violations". In 2017, it shut down Wikipedia.

Turkey remains a tourism destination for Westerners, but now the second aspect of border control came to the fore: policing what foreigners can see while they are in the country.

Pat Yale, a Cambridge University graduate, moved to Turkey in 1998 and began living in a

CREDIT: Neil Julian/PicFair

cave-house in Cappadocia. "For anyone moving to Turkey from a country such as the UK, the single biggest barrier to accessing knowledge has to be the Turkish language," she told Index.

"This is especially the case with bureaucratic language, which is notoriously difficult even for native speakers to understand; when translated, it all too often ends up reading like gobbledygook. Of course, language issues render libraries fairly useless for newcomers. In this context it hardly helps that Wikipedia has been banned in Turkey for more than two years."

Despite problems accessing information, Yale managed to write for the Lonely Planet Guide and co-authored four other English books on Turkey. Nowadays, she advises travellers to prepare for information restrictions before reaching the Turkish border. "I'm not much of a techie myself, but the obvious advice in general is to sign up to a VPN to get round the blocks," Yale added. To get around the Wikipedia ban, she devised a different technique: putting an "e" before Wikipedia in the address bar. "I absolutely hate not having

access to the site," she said.

Turkey's border with Syria is 822km; its border with Iraq is about 330km. For activists, writers, researchers and journalists such as Yale on their way to Turkey, recent stories from those borders were alarming. Since the Syrian civil war began in 2011, and especially after the rise of Isis and the flourishing of Kurdish-controlled cantons in 2013, Turkey's borders with Iraq and Syria moved to the centre of Turkish politics. Security forces, which for years failed to detect and detain Isis and Kurdish militants heading to Syria and northern Iraq, are more vigorous nowadays.

Some journalists, such as Steve Sweeney, have found getting into Turkey an issue. →

ABOVE: Tourists take photographs inside the Hagia Sophia mosque in Istanbul, Turkey, but they cannot have access to its Wikipedia page in Turkey

When borders alienate more than protect, they no longer serve their proper purpose

→ The international editor at the London-based socialist newspaper Morning Star, Sweeney arrived at Istanbul's Sabiha Gökçen Airport in March 2019 and was immediately detained by border police. "A police officer grabbed my phone out of my hand and bundled me into a holding area next to their office," Sweeney wrote in a piece detailing his detainment. "The tiny smoke-filled room was already packed when I arrived. The 18 men looked puzzled and surprised at my arrival . I was the only person of non-Turkish or Middle Eastern appearance."

After a brief interrogation, the border police told Sweeney that he was a national security threat. Sweeney was put on a Pegasus Airlines flight to London. He is now on a blacklist and is banned from entering Turkey. Around the time of Sweeney's detention, two French Communist Party members experienced a similar ordeal.

Turkish border police are wary of writers and activists such as Sweeney who visit Turkish border cities to communicate with fellow-minded activists for political or journalistic purposes. Some of the fears of border authorities are hardly unfounded: over the past half-decade, hundreds of Isis militants from the USA and the EU have passed through Turkey on their way to Raqqa. But those border risks and past mistakes now allow the Turkish authorities to bar critical voices from entering the country. Over the past three years, about a dozen correspondents have learned they've been blacklisted from Turkey while trying to cross the border. Border police

handed them notices, put them on planes and sent them back.

Yale, who is now working on a book about Gertrude Bell's travels in Anatolia, acknowledges that borders have long been problematic in a geography as politically troubled as Turkey. Bell, an ardent traveller who advised Winston Churchill (the British statesman who later became prime minister of the UK), helped draw up the borders of the Middle East after World War I.

"Foreigners newly arrived in a country obviously vary in how much prior knowledge they have of it," Yale said. "But one risk is that we bring with us a set of assumptions about how things work based on what happens in our own countries."

Our own intellectual borders can hide vital information about countries we travel to. Yale advises visitors to Turkey to prepare by using social media as a reference point.

"In the face of these problems, the various websites and Facebook sites set up specifically to link foreigners with each other can be invaluable. They enable people to ask questions of those who've recently dealt with the same problems or whose longer stays in the country mean that they may have a better understanding of the language and the different systems in operation."

But therein lies a conundrum. According to Freedom House's 2018 Freedom on the Net report, Turkey is among five countries that showed the largest decline in internet freedom in the past five years. It argued that it left social media companies with little choice "but to censor non-violent political commentary as a condition of doing business in the country". Others argue that they have other choices.

Changing the status of Turkey from a bridge to a border between East and West has come at this steep price. When borders alienate more than protect, they no longer serve their proper purpose, as disgruntled locals join expats in looking beyond borders for lives elsewhere. ⊗

Kaya Genç is a contributing editor for Index on Censorship (Turkey)

CREDIT: Jehad Awrtani/Cartoon Movement

Culture can "challenge" disinformation

By closing the Mediterranean border governments are seeking to cut us off from each other. **Irene Caselli** travels to Lampedusa to talk to artists trying to tell migrants' stories

48(03): 11/13 | DOI: 10.1177/0306422019876435

ITALY MARKS ITS National Day of Remembrance for the Victims of Immigration on 3 October, but as its government becomes increasingly hostile towards migration and Europe's borders are getting more impenetrable, voices in support of migrants are dwindling.

This is where artistic initiatives are coming to the fore – shedding light on the plight of those trying to make it across the Mediterranean and the ideas that they bring with them.

On the island of Lampedusa, Giacomo Sferlazzo has taken wood from the boats which carried migrants and is carving it into puppets.

They will be used in a show which is due to premiere later in the year and will focus on positive multicultural encounters in contrast to the hostile political rhetoric.

He is revisiting Sicily's Opera dei Pupi, which is one of its cultural traditions. Now recognised by Unesco, the Opera dei Pupi dates back to the early 19th century and traditionally used puppets to tell the stories of Christian knights fighting against the Moors over control of the Mediterranean.

"My idea is to relate the potential for encounter that is already present in the traditional Pupi," said Sferlazzo.

To do this he will transform the clash between cultures in the traditional shows into an exchange between cultures.

The show will tell the story of a Tunisian boy arriving in Italy to look for work. He says that using wood from the boats shows how porous borders can be when art gives new relevance to objects such as these.

"Memory is not neutral, it is a political act," he said. "One chooses what to remember and what to forget.

"Wood's memory is somewhat magic: from the felled tree to the carving, the treatment, until it is transformed into a boat, which sets sail with people onboard, eventually ending up in the dump and becoming rubbish. That's when I arrive, giving yet another life to this piece of wood."

Lampedusa is key to understanding the background for this work. It is under the administration of the Italian region of Sicily, but it is close to the coasts of Tunisia and for decades it has represented the frontline in the arrival of migrants into Europe.

It was here where, in 2013, one of the worst tragedies took place. A boat carrying more than 500 people caught fire half a mile off the island's most iconic beach and 366 people died. The event was reported around the world and it became a turning point for Europe's migration policies. In 2016, the anniversary was made into a national day of remembrance.

Europe's strict migration policies go back several years, but things have worsened since Italy's current government took power last year. Matteo Salvini, of the far-right Lega party and still deputy prime minister as Index went to press, has regularly lambasted migrant rescue operations in the Mediterranean. He has also said that Italy will not be used as a refugee camp by the rest of the European Union, and a law has just been passed by the Italian →

Today we need more reflection – we need to turn art into something that makes you think

Creativity makes it possible to knock down barriers and for ideas to circulate more freely

→ parliament that any NGO vessel entering Italian waters without permission faces a fine of up to €1m ($1.12 million).

So far in 2019 the number of migrants reaching Italy's shores (2,779 by the end of June) has been much lower than the peak in 2017, when 83,752 arrived.

But the death rate on the central Mediterranean route has shot up, from a yearly average of 2% in 2016 (4,049 believed missing or dead out of 201,097 departures from Libya) to nearly 7% so far this year (972 from 14,335 total departures), according to the Institute for International Political Studies (ISPI), an Italian think-tank.

Matteo Villa, head of ISPI's migration programme, says that many of the deaths are because of the lack of government and NGO rescue operations at sea.

He adds that culture can play a big role in challenging disinformation and anti-migrant rhetoric. He cites as an example the Our Boat project, displayed at this year's Venice Biennale. It was the wreckage of a fishing boat on which hundreds of migrants died in 2015 when it capsized and sank off the coast of Libya. The boat was later recovered by Italian authorities and given to Swiss-Icelandic artist Christoph Büchel, who had the idea for the project. After the Biennale ends in November, the boat is due to be brought back to the Sicilian port of Augusta to become an open-air museum.

But Sferlazzo says that art should stay away from easy sentimentalism. "For us it is fundamental to keep alive the memory of something that is still happening, with a critical perspective," he told Index. "Today's artist has to put together feelings with data, because otherwise all there is left is a carnival of emotions. Today we need more reflection – we need to turn art into something that makes you think."

Together with the political collective

Askavusa, the Lampedusa-born artist is behind several projects aimed at raising awareness around migration. For example, the collective has set up a museum of migration that displays objects carried by migrants when arriving on the island.

Lampedusa as a symbolic border is at the heart of the work of writer and theatre director Davide Enia, who spent several months there. He spoke to NGO workers, locals, members of the coastguard, volunteers and migrants themselves. His book, Notes on a Shipwreck, came out in 2017 and circles around migration although the word "migrant" never appears.

He retells the story of a young man, born in Morocco and raised in Italy, who spoke with a perfect Roman accent. He had been arrested as a minor for stealing a wallet and sent back to Morocco, where he did not know the language or have any family. Upon arriving in Lampedusa, after surviving the trip on the boat, he surprised all the volunteers because he sounded Italian.

"The borders that need to stay open are those relating to human beings," said Enia. "Opening up the ports means opening up to the relationships and the interchanges that are the basis of life on this planet." The book was turned into a theatre show, The Abyss, which is touring Italy this autumn, with international dates in Brussels for late October and a date in Lampedusa on 4 October.

The 3 October tragedy was also the reason why Emanuela Pistone, a professional actor and director, decided to use art as a therapeutic space for migrants who had arrived in the

CREDIT: Ignacio Pereyra

ABOVE: Giacomo
Sferlazzo inside the
Museum of Migration

Sicilian port of Catania, her hometown. Following the Lampedusa shipwreck and another off Catania in August of the same year, she founded the Liquid Company theatre troupe.

She started working with some of the survivors of the Catania shipwreck, trying to provide a distraction and overcome trauma. The experiment turned into something more stable and the group staged four original plays on the issues of human trafficking, the asylum system and the struggles of migrants. Their original stories and texts are turned into scripts, but all start off with a joint experiment.

For example, members of the troupe read the Universal Declaration of Human Rights during rehearsals.

"The first time we read them out loud, after we had already studied them, several people started laughing out loud after every article. One of the guys said: 'Nothing that is in there is true'."

Pistone explains that these young men and women felt their human rights and dignity had been denied by Europe's hard borders. All had risked their lives by travelling through the Sahara desert, many had survived Libyan jails and then they crossed the Mediterranean in rickety boats. The laughing scene eventually became part of one of the Liquid Company shows.

Beyond the artistic value of the production, says Pistone, what is important is that creativity makes it possible to knock down barriers and for ideas to circulate more freely.

"Creative activities manage to connect people through emotional relationships and sensitive communication. You connect empathically, no matter where you are from – you manage to overcome any kind of barrier." ⊗

Irene Caselli is a contributing editor for Index on Censorship magazine. She is based in Monte Castello di Vibio, Italy

Lines of duty

One of the few foreign journalists to regularly visit Yemen, **Laura Silvia Battaglia**, talks about the challenges of getting in

48(03):14/15 I DOI: 10.1177/0306422019876436

IN THE PAST, navigating checkpoints used to be a key difficulty for journalists reporting from a war zone. These days, the difficulty is how to actually get to those checkpoints, because not all wars are accessible to those wishing to document them.

Countries are using visas as a way of controlling the entry of international journalists to conflict zones – particularly Syria. The restrictions there are driving more reporters to try to enter the country through the more porous Turkish border, but from 2012 to late 2013, as long as you arranged a ferryman with one of the anti-Bashar al-Assad rebel militias, your place on the frontline was guaranteed.

Such passage – which could still prove dangerous – shaped a great deal of the anti-Assad narrative on the Syrian conflict, particularly for the first three years of the war, which started in 2011.

Assad's government realised this a little too late, but for the past two years it's been easier for journalists to get government-issued visas than it was seven years ago.

Having learned from this "lesson", other governments have changed tack. Iraq, for example, opened its borders to anyone wishing to enter the country to cover the Mosul offensive in 2016-2017.

Access was through Erbil airport, in northern Iraq – also known as Iraqi Kurdistan – and Europeans, Americans and many other nationalities did not need visas. Checkpoints to get in and out of Mosul were probably the easiest to navigate in the whole of Iraq.

If you had the right permit and the correct paperwork, the coalition forces (the Iraqi and Peshmerga armies) would assure you a smooth passage. This was no longer true by the end of the offensive, in July 2017, by which time the government had announced it had regained control of Mosul and defeated Isis. Although pockets of fighting continued in the city and lives continued to be lost, journalists were encouraged not to enter Mosul between specified hours and told to wait at checkpoints for something to happen.

The official version was that it was for our safety, although one of the main reasons was to prevent international media workers from witnessing the extra-judicial executions of suspected Isis snipers – executions which violated their rights as prisoners of war and for which the Iraqi authorities were right to fear criticism.

Interestingly, when it comes to issuing visas for Baghdad, the Iraqi government is much stricter and the no-go area now starts from Basra, frequently the site of anti-government protests, the oppression of political activists, police and militia action, and local government corruption. Basra doesn't need witnesses.

Yemen, on the other hand, home of the the most under-reported conflict in the Middle East, has outdone all its neighbours, largely on account of there being so few land routes into the country. During the four years of its current civil war, it has been almost impossible for foreign journalists to get in.

The extremely weak Yemeni government has issued very few visas, which are the only

BELOW: Laura Silvia Battaglia (right) and Iraqi journalist Halan Ibrahim Shehka (left) in Al Kut, Iraq

Not all wars are accessible to those wishing to document them

CREDITS: (right) International Journalism Festival, Perugia, Italy and (left) Laura Silvia Battaglia

way of gaining independent access to the country. Even when this problem is overcome, it's still not easy, or economically feasible, for a foreign journalist to get to Yemen.

There are the options of travelling by sea from Djibouti to the port of Aden, with the risk of being attacked by pirates or long delays while equipment is checked. The alternative is going via Oman, where travelling overland means spending hundreds of dollars to drive north for two days and passing through nearly 40 checkpoints, some of which are controlled by al-Qaeda.

For international media workers, the easiest option is the most expensive one: flying. But only with the country's national carrier, Yemenia. They have very few flights from Amman, Cairo and Khartoum to Yemen, charging exorbitant prices (more than €1,000 for a compulsory return ticket to be paid in US dollars – cash – and purchased at one of the airline's official agencies with no assurance that there will be an economy class and no guarantee that the plane will actually leave on the specified date). This also explains why many foreign journalists prefer, for both logistical and financial reasons, to rely on Saudi media tours which are organised in meticulous detail from Riyadh, offering all necessary services to secure a breaking news story: a day on the Ma'rib frontline, south of Sana'a; a visit to an orphanage of former Houthi child soldiers; meeting victims of torture in Houthi prisons; and talking to the authorities of Ma'rib, the only governorate recovering both socially and economically and under the protection of Saudi troops.

Reports from Yemen tend to be fairly similar. There's one trump card, though, and it makes reporting in Yemen a primarily female affair. Women, both local and foreign, provided they dress like local women and are accompanied by a local man, can cross checkpoints with relative ease. They are rarely asked for their papers and their bags are almost never checked – largely because the checkpoints are operated by men, who are not permitted to touch women.

The extremely weak Yemeni government has issued very few visas, which are the only way of gaining independent access to the country

This was standard procedure during the first two years of the conflict, although over the past year, central government authorities have stepped up security and added female personnel at checkpoints. Nevertheless, once you get into Yemen – if you have the right paperwork, know what you're doing and are familiar with the place and the culture – as a female reporter, it isu still much easier than if you are a man. ⊛

ABOVE: Laura Silvia Battaglia speaking at the International Journalism Festival in Perugia, Italy

Translated by **Denise Muir**

Laura Silvia Battaglia is the contributing editor for Index on Censorship (Iraq and Yemen)

Locking the gates

The USA is making it much harder for artists, writers, musicians and academics to gain access to the country. **Jan Fox** finds an atmosphere of fear where people self-censor because they fear being turned back at the border

48(03): 16/18 | DOI: 10.1177/0306422019876437

THE POLITICAL WRANGLE over immigration to the USA has all eyes fixed on its southern border and the proposed Mexican wall to keep people out. But US controls are tighter on every border with the consequence that the country is in danger of shutting out ideas. And what is the implication for freedom of expression if we can no longer hear the voices of visiting artists, musicians, writers and academics from around the world?

"It's alarming," said Summer Lopez, senior director of free expression programmes for PEN. "Pre-[President Donald] Trump we had to worry about increased surveillance of writers around the world and how we felt about that in the US. This feeds into what we're seeing now with new visa policies such as social media collection, which has a chilling effect on freedom of expression."

Almost all US visa applicants are now asked for their social media information for the last five years including user names for sites such as Facebook, Twitter and YouTube. Even applicants for the USA's visa waiver programme, the Esta, are asked to provide this information, though for them it is not yet obligatory.

Matthew Covey, of Tamizdat, a New York-based non-profit organisation that promotes international cultural mobility and exchange, says it's a worrying development. Although there is little evidence the government is using social media profiles to deny entry, it does not stop artists and performers from self-censoring.

"I recently had an inquiry from a Norwegian opera singer who was panicked about the delay in her visa in case the delay was due to her social media. She had posted her opinions about [the] Standing Rock [protest], and it was the fact that she panicked and had removed the posts from her Facebook page that is significant for free speech.

"This fear, perhaps way more powerful than the reality itself, is a concern, especially when you think about the interconnectedness of intelligence – for example Homeland Security and Interpol data. There's the question: if the US government is collecting all this information on me, where else is it going?"

It's also creating fear in the academic world, says Sarah McLaughlin, of the Foundation for Individual Rights in Education, where academics worry they may be denied entry for something they have put on Facebook or Twitter.

"Academics may choose to self-censor rather than risk engaging in speech they believe could limit their ability to study here," she said. "Worse, as it's unclear how this information is used, there is the possibility that the government may use the information it collects to scour academics' social media posts for objectionable views. Both of these are inappropriate results in a country committed to free expression."

The Trump travel ban, introduced in 2017 and still in effect, is something else that has had a detrimental impact on creative voices from outside the country. "The travel ban was a tipping point. It said, 'You're not welcome here' and was such a symbolic move that it's hard to come back from and has long-term effects," said Lopez. "Other perspectives are very important for Americans. We need to hear creative voices from Yemen, Syria, Iran and Libya – and if we can't, that's alarming."

She says that Kareem Abeed, the Syrian producer of the Oscar-nominated documentary

CREDIT: Andrew Caballero-Reynolds/AFP/Getty

Last Men in Aleppo, about the current Syrian civil war, was refused a visa to attend the 2018 ceremony. He finally got one with the help of PEN after there was an uproar.

And there's a darker implication stemming from the ban. Joy Garnett, arts advocacy officer at the National Coalition Against Censorship, told Index: "The direct adverse effect on international artists and writers may be hard to measure precisely but it should be to everyone's concern that artists who have previously looked towards the US as a place where they can express themselves freely run a greater risk of being exposed to retaliation under repressive regimes at home when the US closes its doors to them."

Academics are also being affected by tighter visa restrictions. FIRE highlights two cases this year where visas were denied to Palestinian speakers who were scheduled to speak at US universities. One was politician and negotiator Hanan Ashrawi (who has been a frequent

visitor to the USA for decades) and the other was Palestinian activist Omar Barghouti, who had been due to speak at colleges including Harvard and New York University. No concrete reasons for the denials were given.

McLaughlin told Index: "One of the great promises American universities can offer students and academics is the possibility of freedom to study and research without government interference or punishment. That freedom is threatened if immigration restrictions are →

ABOVE: A security officer observes from inside an office at the US Immigration and Customs Enforcement (ICE), which forms part of the Department of Homeland Security in Washington DC, October 2017

That freedom is threatened if immigration restrictions are used to interfere with the free exchange of ideas across borders

Academics may choose to self-censor rather than risk engaging in speech they believe could limit their ability to study here

→ used to interfere with the free exchange of ideas across borders."

Similar refusals have affected visiting Chinese professors and scholars, possibly due to heightened fears of espionage and political theft. A New York Times article in April 2019 highlighted the case of Chinese professor of international relations Zhu Feng, whose visa was cancelled by FBI agents at the airport on a recent visit to Los Angeles.

There are many reasons why visas are denied, explains Covey. "Often people just have the wrong visa. They come in on an Esta, but really need an O or P work visa. [Other visa types apply to academics.] The authorities have turned a blind eye to much of this in previous years – for example, the loophole of the 'audition' or 'showcase' criteria where, for instance, musicians may be able to perform at a one-off festival – but now customs and border control enforcement has really tightened up.

"This administration is buried in xenophobia and hysteria, although there's been a general tightening of the screws on visas since the 1990s so it's not all Trump. With the xenophobia aspects it's hard to keep track of the fact that most of the immigration rules are, in fact, about labour, not security. They were originally designed not to take jobs away from Americans. And if you're an artist who says you'll work for free just to be seen, that's also unhelpful as it's deemed that you are lowering the value of US labour," said Covey.

Lack of officer training or having the "wrong" visa, means many artists might be denied entry or experience harassment when they arrive at the border.

One of these was Australian children's author Mem Fox. Despite 116 previous visits to the

USA to promote her books, she was detained and questioned in 2017. Cartoonist Ali Dorani (aka Eaten Fish) who fled Iran, was the winner of a Courage In Cartooning award in 2016 but was denied a visa to visit the USA last year to visit the annual convention of the Association of American Editorial Cartoonists' Convention.

At the 2019 Oscars, Mexican actor Jorge A Guerrero – who was in the multi-nominated film Roma – was denied a visitor visa three times. He missed several awards ceremonies, including the Golden Globes, before finally being admitted just in time for the Oscars ceremony following pressure from distributor Netflix. It's not clear why he was previously denied visas.

Rocketing visa costs are another factor in dissuading foreign creatives who want to visit the USA, says Covey.

"Back in the early 1990s it was affordable and viable, and mostly the paperwork could be filled out by interns at arts organisations. But there's been 'bureaucratic creep' since then," he said. "Two years ago the cost of filing for an O [work] visa went up significantly. In 1992, a five-piece band might have been able to come here for under $500 including all filing fees; today it's ten times that and you usually need a lawyer – this is a real impediment to foreign artists wanting to come."

It may have become too hard for creative people to even try to visit the USA at a time when it's critical to hear other voices, says Lopez.

"After [the New York terror attacks of] 9/11 we worked hard at PEN to ensure international cultural exchange," she said. "The spread of nationalism and isolationism around the world means this is exponentially more important. We are hearing exclusive nationalist messages and we are not hearing from people with different perspectives, so this is very disruptive. We at PEN are fighting for that space to hear other voices. What's going on now definitely increases the sense of alarm." ⊗

Jan Fox is the US contributing editor for Index on Censorship. She is based in Los Angeles

Reaching for the off switch

Governments around the world, including democratic ones, are increasingly using internet shutdowns during elections and at moments of political crisis. **Meera Selva** investigates

48(03): 19/22 I DOI: 10.1177/0306422019876438

IN JUNE THIS year, faced with hundreds of protesters in the streets, Sudan's military government reached for old and new solutions. It opened fire on civilians outside a military headquarters in Khartoum calling for democracy. It closed down the internet to stop more coming to take their places.

Then in August, the Indian government shut down mobile and broadband services in the parts of Kashmir under its jurisdiction as it announced plans to remove the region's special status, essentially cutting the autonomy of the area and putting it under direct control of central government.

India is the country that has written the handbook on internet shutdowns. Other countries are reading it. India has restricted access to the internet during periods of unrest since 2010 and the duration and frequency has increased dramatically since the Narendra Modi-led government came to power in 2014.

It is now the country that shuts down the internet more than any other, with 134 shutdowns recorded last year. The government previously shut internet access in Kashmir for 133 days in 2016, according to research group InternetShutdowns, but this latest digital blackout, accompanied by an unprecedented removal of political sovereignty, is a clear example of how internet access is being used to wield political power.

Closing down the internet is increasingly being used as a reaction by countries around the world when protests arise or elections get controversial.

The move in Sudan came in a moment of massive upheaval that began in December 2018 with protests over the tripling of the price of bread and led, in April 2019, to President Omar al-Bashir stepping down after 30 years. The military government that replaced him, the Transitional Military Council, found itself directly at odds with the well-educated, digitally-savvy protestors who wanted to make sure that this council made way for a fully democratic government. They ignored a curfew the council had tried to impose in Khartoum and stayed on the →

Half the world's population is now online, so internet control is becoming more powerful as a way to control civil society

CREDIT: Sara Qaed/Cartoon Movement

→ streets, demanding a democratic transition.

On 3 June, the military council opened fire, killing more than 100 protestors and implementing an internet blackout, citing security concerns. The blockade stopped protestors from mobilising and allowed the military council to carry out extra-judicial killings and detain protestors with impunity.

Data from digital advocacy group Access Now shows the number of internet shutdowns worldwide rose from 75 in 2016 to 196 in 2018, and the number is rising again in 2019.

Of the 196 shutdowns in 2018, governments used reasons of public safety to justify 91 of them and national security for another 40. In reality, 98 shutdowns were triggered at times of political instability and protest.

In 2019 many governments that had not tended to try to get people offline discovered the off switch. These countries included Benin, which turned off the internet during parliamentary elections in 2019 and Malawi, where people found themselves unable to get in online in the jours after a tightly contested presidential election.

Social media blackouts are a quick way to put obstacles in the way of collective behaviour, says Silvia Majo-Vazquez, a researcher at the Reuters Institute for the Study of Journalism. "Groups can, of course, use other channels to organise, but the scale of mobilisation is quicker on social media than on other channels, which is why authorities seek to block it."

This is especially true in Sudan, where only 28% of the population is online and their demographic coincides closely with the demographic of protestors.

Half the world's population is now online, so internet control is becoming more powerful as a way to control civil society. Berhan Taye, of Access Now, said: "Part of this is that governments don't understand how to combat misinformation and think shutdowns help. But in places like Sudan it is also clear we had forgotten people-power, and the impact people gathering can have. And governments think they can use shutdowns to mitigate that."

One trend in 2019 has been the tendency of more democratic countries, including Benin, to use shutdowns around election time and times of civic unrest.

The UK shut down internet access on London's underground rail network during climate change protests in April, affecting thousands of people who had travelled across the country to join the march.

CREDIT: RobinOlimb/ iStock

BY THE NUMBERS

Increasingly countries shut down the internet at times of crisis

20 DAYS

In the Democratic Republic of Congo, the government shut down the internet for **20 days** during an election in 2018

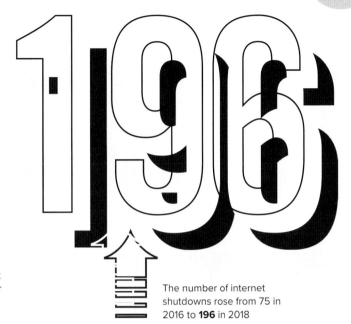

The number of internet shutdowns rose from 75 in 2016 to **196** in 2018

Source: Access Now

Mary Meeker, the former Morgan Stanley analyst and venture capitalist who has tracked digital trends since 1995, says that fewer and fewer people worldwide live in countries with zero internet censorship – 20% in 2018 compared with 24% in 2016.

And states are developing better technologies to do it. Even countries such as Ethiopia, with a low internet-access rate, can access deep packet inspection technology to limit internet access in some regions. This technology is a form of data processing that looks at the type of data being sent over the internet and reroutes it accordingly.

The technology was also used this year in Egypt to block websites set up by campaigners who wanted to oppose President Abdel Fattah el-Sisi's plans to hold a referendum to change the constitution and allow him to stay in power until 2030. The campaigners set up a petition that gained more than 700,000 signatures, only to see it blocked within hours.

Egyptian journalist Dahlia Kholaif has documented the use of internet blackouts in Sinai, where shutdowns are accompanied by a clampdown on civil society, including imprisoning cyber activists for a host of crimes such as threatening national security, contempt of religion and spreading false information.

This year, she says, the government has made it clear it is willing to choke communications across the whole country, not just Sinai.

"This is a government that knows the strength of social media. It came to power through social media and has now spent a lot of time and money making sure it can get it under control," she said. "This is the worst it has ever been."

There is also more justification. Fake news, concerns over national security and concerns over the rapid spread of hate speech online have all created spaces and justifications for governments. In Sri Lanka, in the wake of the 2019 Easter attacks, the government suspended social media. This was ostensibly to stop the spread of hate speech that could rebound on the →

The UK shut down internet access on London's underground rail network during climate change protests in April

For a while he was the only civilian in the country who could get online via his mobile

→ country's Muslim communities, but in reality the ban also helped stopped discussion of the intelligence failures that led to the attack.

Technology and mobile companies have been slow to develop norms that make it clear when governments have the right to shut down the internet.

This is particularly true in sub-Saharan Africa and much of the global south, where mobile data is how people primarily get online. In February 2019, 54% of all web traffic in Africa and 60% in Asia was via mobiles. In Europe, it was 39%.

In the Democratic Republic of Congo, the government shut down access to the internet for 20 days after a disputed presidential election in December 2018. The country's two main mobile operators, Vodafone and Orange, said they had to comply under the terms of their operating licences.

Catherine Gicheru, who works in civic technology and data journalism in Code for Africa, which helps citizens use the internet for political engagement, argues that telecoms companies should use their influence more.

"These telcos are multinationals, and yes, they operate within the laws of a country, but why can't they have the guts to stand up and say 'no' sometimes?" she said.

Gicheru calls for an international code of conduct for telecoms companies clearly stating they will not sign licensing deals that give political authorities the right to order them to switch off their signals at will.

This would help mobile operators navigate situations such as that in Zimbabwe, where the government shut down the internet at the start of the year during civilian protests, only for the country's courts to reverse the move a

week later, ruling that the authorities had overreached themselves.

Strive Masiyiwa, the head of Econet, one of the country's main mobile providers, apologised on his Facebook page for the shutdown and said the company had no choice but to comply.

It should also help avoid odd rulings such as the one in Sudan in June 2019, when lawyer Abdel-Adheem Hassan won a lawsuit against the telecoms operator Zain Sudan over the internet shutdown – but the court ruled that the suit applied only to him. For a while he was the only civilian in the country who could get online via his mobile.

"One advantage of filing lawsuits against shutdowns is that it creates some transparency over who exactly issued the order and how long it will last," said Taye.

Ultimately, the power to end internet shutdowns may lie with the technology companies themselves. Google's sister company, Loon, is developing giant internet balloons designed to deliver internet connectivity to remote parts of east Africa and they have already been used to connect people hit by flooding in parts of Latin America, including Peru. Facebook, meanwhile, is developing the use of drones to get remote areas online.

So far, neither of these companies has used its new technology to allow citizens to bypass government-mandated internet shutdowns, but they have raised awareness of digital rights.

And as research groups such as the Brookings Institute assess the exact cost of internet shutdowns to the economy of a country, corporations and citizens may well be persuaded to exert more pressure on governments – and technology companies and mobile operators – to clarify when it is not acceptable to cut off the flow of information. And that may discourage governments from continuing to reach for the off switch when things get rough. ⊗

Meera Selva *is director of the journalism fellowship programme at the Reuters Institute for the Study of Journalism at the University of Oxford*

Hiding your true self

Crossing borders can be dangerous if you are an LGBT person. **Mark Frary** investigates what to do to keep safe

48(03): 23/25 | DOI: 10.1177/0306422019876455

IN JANUARY THIS year, LGBT people and their allies around the world celebrated as Angola announced a new penal code that finally removed references to "vices against nature" – widely interpreted as a ban on homosexual conduct.

Angola's decriminalisation is yet another landmark achievement in the recognition of LGBT rights around the world. However, advances such as this hide the fact that at a border, if you end up being stopped, they are going to be googling your name and seeing if you are on Facebook and other social media to find out as much as possible.

In its comprehensive report on the status of LGBT rights around the world – State-Sponsored Homophobia 2019 – the International Lesbian, Gay, Bisexual, Trans and Intersex Association (ILGA) shows that at least 32 UN member states have introduced or interpreted provisions to restrict the freedom of expression in relation to sexual orientation and gender identity issues.

The ILGA report's lead author, Lucas Ramón Mendos, said: "On the one hand, we are moving forward in a progressive way, removing barriers. We see countries like Mongolia, South Korea and the Philippines moving towards more protective legal frameworks while in Africa we have seen incredible progress in Mozambique and Angola. On the other hand, some countries are backtracking, enacting laws that restrict the dissemination of ideas or communications among LGBT people."

The introduction to the report highlights some of the successes achieved since it was last published in 2017. These include India striking anti-gay sections from its penal code, Ireland appointing Leo Varadkar as its first openly gay head of state, the World Health Organisation striking gender incongruence from its list of mental disorders, and Botswana making it easier for transpeople to change their official genders.

Yet, despite this optimism, there is cause for concern that while legislation targeting LGBT people around the world is being dismantled, the reality on the ground is very different.

"We see that there are countries that are protective against sexual orientation but that doesn't mean the situation is safe on the ground," said Mendos.

The report reveals that cases involving freedom of expression are one of the most common type of complaint handled by UN treaty bodies, coming second only to issues involving LGBT asylum seekers. Russia, which introduced its "gay propaganda law" in 2013, and former Soviet republics are the countries were LGBT rights are some of the worst.

Saul Shanagher, of travel safety →

THE DANGER ZONES

Each year, gay travel publication Spartacus publishes a Gay Travel Index which ranks countries on the risks they pose to LGBT travellers. The index takes into account national legislation, LGBT+ rights, religious influence and HIV travel restrictions as well as whether locals are hostile and whether Pride events are banned. For 2019, the worst ranked countries are as follows:

1 The Russian republic of Chechnya
2 Somalia
3 Saudi Arabia
4 Iran
5 Yemen
6 United Arab Emirates
7 Libya
8 Afghanistan
9 Qatar
10 Malawi

CREDIT: Ogla Maltseva/AFP/Getty

→ consultancy be Travelwise, said: "Everything is often fine when crossing the border. Then you have a run-in with a local who takes offence and calls law enforcement and they have to be seen to be doing something about it. It is a personal choice, but are you prepared to hide who you are?"

Hiding your sexual orientation may not come easily.

The company's LGBT travel adviser, Jeremy Wilkes, says many of his generation did not come out until they were in their late 20s and have had experience of being discreet.

"The kids now don't necessarily have those skills. They want to say who they are and be themselves," he said.

Global telecommunications company Vodafone takes its responsibility for employees, who it sends on more than 40,000 business trips every year, very seriously. The company, which regularly appears in Stonewall's list of top global employers of LGBT staff, owns and operates mobile networks in 25 countries, including some in which homosexuality is criminalised.

The company's travel security manager, David Jovic, says many of its LGBT employees choose to be more secretive about their personal lives when travelling, although this can be easier said than done.

"Avoiding public displays of affection that may be perceived negatively in certain locations is essential and can usually be avoided rather easily. More complicated is making sure not to share personal details about oneself that might give your sexual orientation away. We are fully cognisant that not being fully transparent about one's personal life and having the feeling one has to hide part of who [one is] can be psychologically taxing."

A person's social media presence can also come under scrutiny. Wilkes said: "At a border, if you end up being stopped, they are going to be googling your name and seeing if you are on Facebook and other social media to find out as much as possible. Our advice is never to give your password or your phone's passcode up at the border, and ask to speak to a consular official."

Jovic added: "Something as simple as disabling notifications on a smartphone can go a long way towards keeping your sexual orientation private. More importantly, making sure your social activity is not visible to your local hosts is critical. It is customary, for completely innocuous reasons, for hosts to make requests to be included in your social networks and it is best to think twice before accepting them."

Dating apps themselves are also encouraging

Something as simple as disabling notifications on a smartphone can go a long way towards keeping your sexual orientation private

LEFT: Protesters confront the authorities at a gay pride rally in Saint Petersburg, Russia, during August 2017. Russia and former Soviet republics threaten the free expression of LGBT people the most, according to complaints handled by UN treaty bodies

Netherlands in 2016 and 500 in Finland between autumn 2015 and February 2017.

Volker Türk, the assistant high commissioner for protection at the UN refugee agency UNHCR says that asylum seekers' right to freedom of expression is often "unduly restricted".

"The journey to safety can prove particularly treacherous for many LGBTI refugees who continue to face prejudice and violence in countries of transit and host countries," he said.

"Officials involved in the process of determination of refugee status and in managing reception conditions should receive sensitive and culturally appropriate training on sexual orientation, gender identity and sex characteristics."

Türk says that even in locations where such refugees are more accepted, and services are accessible, many choose to conceal their sexual orientation and gender identity for fear they might be targeted or marginalised.

The advances made on the international stage are impressive, but they also hide what is happening within countries. ILGA's Mendos said: "With the United States, for example, we are aware of the nuances between the legal process in each of the 50 states. In some there is no legal protection against discrimination and there is the ridiculous situation where someone can get married on Friday but then get fired on the Monday."

The strides made in the recognition of LGBT rights have been enormous in recent years and should be celebrated. Yet reports from a number of countries show that LGBT people are still having their freedom of expression curtailed. ✖

travellers to hide their sexual orientation and gender identity status. In 2014, the Grindr app warned users in Egypt to hide their identities on social media. In an on-screen message it warned that the country's police were posing as being LGBT to entrap the popular app's users. As a result, it changed its app so that users in Egypt and countries such as Russia, Saudi Arabia and Zimbabwe automatically had their locations hidden by default.

In July 2019, dating app Tinder rolled out a feature called Traveller Alert which hides users' profiles until they return home from one of the 70 or so countries where homosexuality is criminalised.

It is not just travellers who are having their freedom of expression restricted. LGBT refugees presenting themselves at international borders face particular challenges.

There are currently no official statistics that assess the number of asylum seekers based on sexual orientation or gender issues, but a 2017 report by the European Union Agency for Fundamental Rights revealed that up to 1,000 people sought asylum with claims linked to sexual orientation and gender identity issues in the

Mark Frary is a journalist and author. He wrote De/Cipher, a guide to cryptography

They shall not pass

Those who criticise governments or cover controversial subjects are increasingly stopped at borders in the USA, Mexico and Cuba. What are the implications? asks **Stephen Woodman**

48(03): 26/28 I DOI: 10.1177/0306422019876440

OFFICIALS IN CALIFORNIA detained US citizen Hugo Castro, a migrant rights activist, as he crossed the border from Mexico for a medical appointment. The agents held Castro for more than five hours and interrogated him about the Central American migrant caravans arriving in Mexico. They also conducted a search of his mobile phone without a warrant, unlocking his photos, emails and social media accounts.

"They were looking for the basis to set up a criminal case," Castro told Index. "The US government wants to charge [activists] with helping people cross the border. Any assistance you provide could lead to charges."

Castro's screening last year was not an isolated incident but part of an international drive to use borders to stem the free flow of information. Journalists and activists are increasingly pulled aside with demands to access their social media accounts.

In recent years, authorities in the USA, Mexico and Cuba have stirred up fear around borders – harassing travellers who document or oppose government abuses. Freedom of expression specialists now worry that the overall impact of a swathe of harsh measures at these borders and others could result in people reining in their speech and involvement in protest because of worries that it will prevent them from travelling.

Digital security expert Ela Stapley (see p32) who worked as a journalist in Mexico for five years, said: "People are likely to self-censor if they believe that their online criticism of a certain country or government will hinder their chances of obtaining a visa. This is an effective way for governments to try and control what people are saying online and it is one of a number of ways that governments around the world limit freedom of expression."

She added: "Journalists and human rights defenders worry about how best to protect themselves, their families, and also people they are working with or seeking to protect."

A recent report by Amnesty International argued that US President Donald Trump was waging a politically motivated campaign against activists and journalists at the US-Mexican border. The report said border agents had systematically targeted people because of "their protected views or expression". Press freedom groups have also voiced concern about the crackdown, which includes enhanced searches of electronic devices at borders and demands for travellers to hand over their social media passwords.

"[These powers] create a climate in which journalists are operating under suspicion," said Courtney Radsch, advocacy director for the US-based Committee to Protect Journalists.

Three months after Castro's screening, an unidentified Department of Homeland Security official leaked screenshots to the news outlet NBC 7. The documents confirmed the existence of a secret database of individuals the US government had targeted with migratory alerts and secondary screenings and Castro's name was among the 59 on the San Diego region watchlist.

The surveillance measures form part of Operation Secure Line, which monitors migrants and asylum-seekers in Mexico – many of whom arrived in the caravans that began forming in central America in October last year. With the Trump administration turning away thousands of asylum requests, many people are stranded along Mexico's northern border.

US Customs and Border Protection initially claimed the watchlist was a response to a breach of the San Diego border in November last year. But one US photojournalist on the list, Ariana Drehsler, told Index she was not present during

CREDIT: Jorge Duenes/Reuters

that incident. Despite this, she was subjected to three screenings shortly after Christmas. During the third interview, agents asked her to leave her camera and phone outside, and then requested access to her photos. She refused.

In May, CBP reworked its explanation for the surveillance measures. In a letter, the agency justified the watchlist by referencing a federal law which an appeals court has already deemed unconstitutional. That law permits the investigation of "any person who 'encourages' or 'induces'" a migrant to enter the USA.

"That's really disturbing, because we weren't encouraging anyone," Drehsler told Index. "I feel I was transparent. But there is no real transparency coming from their end."

Drehsler has not been stopped while crossing the border since January and is unsure whether the alert is still active, but she is now worried about carrying electronic devices across borders, as doing so might expose her subjects and sources.

In April, two citizen rights groups – the Electronic Frontier Foundation and the American Civil Liberties Union – filed a federal lawsuit against warrantless border searches, which they say have nearly quadrupled since 2015.

Mexican immigration officials have also harassed human rights defenders in response to alerts from US authorities. Nora Phillips, the legal director and co-founder of Al Otro Lado, an organisation providing legal services for asylum-seekers, was denied entry into Mexico at Guadalajara airport on 1 February. She was detained for nine hours with her seven-year-old child and officials provided no food and drink, even when Phillips begged for water so she could swallow the medication she requires for a serious genetic disorder.

> *[These powers] create a climate in which journalists are operating under suspicion. It chills journalists because they are concerned about their ability to protect their sources*

Phillips was sent back to Los Angeles and she has been unable to leave the country since.

"You have [migratory alerts] because there are really dangerous human beings," Phillips told Index. "You don't use them to silence and geographically limit political dissidents."

Amnesty believes the effort to block the entrance of human rights defenders into Mexico appears to be "targeted and co-ordinated", as part of a bi-national US-Mexico initiative that is ostensibly designed to combat human smuggling.

According to Amnesty, the Trump administration is deliberately conflating the concept of humanitarian work with the crime of human smuggling. The organisation says the effort is a breach of international law, which defines a human smuggler as someone who exploits migrants for material gain. On 5 June, two leading migrant rights activists, Irineo Mujica and Cristobal Sánchez, were arrested in Mexico on human smuggling charges. Two days later, Trump announced he was lifting the threat of tariffs on Mexican goods. The president justified the move by citing the "strong measures" Mexico had agreed to take to stem migration. →

ABOVE: A US border patrol agent opens a metal door separating the USA and Mexico in San Ysidro. It is one of the busiest land crossings in the world

ABOVE: A member of the Mexican National Guard patrols the banks of the Rio Bravo at the border between Mexico and the USA in Cludad Juarez, Mexico, July 2019

→ Nevertheless, a Mexican court ordered the release of Mujica and Sánchez the following week. The lawyers for both defendants demonstrated they were hundreds of miles from Mexico's southern border at the time they allegedly took payment for transporting migrants. However, the case remains open and Mujica has suffered police harassment since.

"The authorities want to create panic in the population," Mujica told Index. "They want to deter people from providing humanitarian aid to migrants, even though offering that aid is legal in Mexico."

What is happening in the USA and Mexico is comparable to the politicisation of travelling across borders in other regions of the Americas.

Cuba has long resorted to barring or deporting foreign nationals whose views they don't like. In May, the government expelled two Mexican artists for allegedly trying to "sabotage" the Havana Biennial art exhibition.

However, Cuban authorities most commonly block the free movement of those looking to leave, not enter. Such bans aim to limit the spread of information that reflects negatively on the country's communist regime.

Cuban journalist Yoani Sánchez was denied permission to leave the country on 20 occasions, beginning in 2008. According to

Sánchez, the ban was a retaliation for her blogging, which the government described as part of a "cyberwar" against Cuba. As a result, Sánchez was unable to collect freedom of speech awards in Spain, Austria and the USA. The ban was finally lifted under Cuba's sweeping migration reform in 2013.

"I still have to pass through special controls where security personnel warn me about the opinions I offer in foreign countries," Sánchez told Index. "But I can leave without any greater obstacles."

She says the Cuban authorities still use access-to-travel as a mechanism of control. The reporter Luz Escobar, who works for Sánchez at the independent digital media outlet 14ymedio, has been prohibited from leaving since January 2018. Digital journalist Iliana Hernández is also barred from foreign travel.

However, Sánchez believes the hardening of borders against free expression in the Americas is becoming more futile, as technology opens up new spaces for communication.

That was certainly evident in June, when a Mexican reporter photographed the lifeless bodies of Óscar Alberto Martínez Ramírez, a Salvadoran migrant, and his daughter Valeria, who had drowned trying to swim the Rio Grande into US territory.

The Mexican newspaper La Jornada initially published the image and it spread rapidly on social media before it was republished in newspapers around the world, becoming a grim reminder of the human cost of Trump's policies.

In Cuba, Sánchez promotes the flow of information by offering classes on how to use the internet and how to bypass the island's closely-monitored network.

"Social media has become a meeting point for people separated by migration," she said. "Authorities can try to regulate digital information but it's becoming very difficult to control." ⊗

CREDIT: Daniel Becerril/Reuters

You have [migratory alerts] because there are really dangerous human beings. You don't use them to silence and geographically limit political dissidents

Stephen Woodman *is the contributing editor for Index in Mexico. He is based in Guadalajara*

"UK border policy damages credibility"

Festival directors warn that the new trend of turning writers and artists away at the UK border threatens the nation's understanding of the world as **Charlotte Bailey** reports

48(03): 29/31 | DOI: 10.1177/0306422019876441

CONGOLESE CHOREOGRAPHER AND dancer Faustin Linyekula's show, In Search of Dinozord, tells the violent history of his home country.

The London International Festival of Theatre was keen to bring his internationally renowned ensemble to the UK for a performance in 2018. The production is about their own experiences of war, bringing deeply personal stories to the wider world, including photographs from the prison where their own writer, Antoine Vumilia Muhindo, was incarcerated and tortured.

Kris Nelson, artistic director and CEO of Lift, was therefore shocked when the UK Home Office rejected the application for one of the dancers on the grounds that it should be possible for a UK-based dancer with the skills to perform instead. After an expensive, embarrassing and time-consuming appeal, Lift did manage to get the performer over in time – just. It is getting much harder for people to cross borders – even when they are special guests of major festivals.

"Over the past three years, the UK government has succeeded in brewing a poisonous cocktail: the tightening of short-stay visa regulations mixed with the devastating impact of Brexit dithering on our credibility worldwide," Nick Barley, director of the Edinburgh International Book Festival, told Index.

Deidre Brock, an Edinburgh MP, said: "The hostile environment has created huge concerns over performers visiting the UK and threatens the very existence of some of our world-leading events."

Festival directors and publishers warn that there is a damaging and dangerous trend against the international exchange of ideas and shared understanding, amounting to a form of cultural censorship that risks turning the UK into a no-go area for many artists.

Ra Page, the founder and editorial manager of publishing house Comma Press, told Index: "This is a version of cultural censorship, and it demeans and reduces us, our understanding of the world and our claims to be aware of what is going on in the world.

"The news mostly tells us things we can't relate to. We also need the person behind that. When we deprive ourselves of hearing from writers who are living there we deprive ourselves of their normality, and their ordinary humanity, and everything we can relate to."

Performers including Wazimbo and Sabry Mosbah have had to cancel performances →

Over the past three years, the UK government has succeeded in brewing a poisonous cocktail

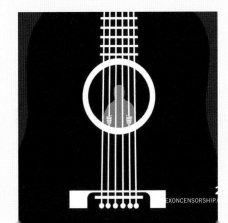

CREDIT: Pete Kreiner / Cartoon Movement

ABOVE: Womad Festival co-founder Peter Gabriel, (pictured right) with musicians Justin Adams and Juldeh Camara, has criticised UK policy that refuses artists entry to the UK to perform

at the Womad music festival, and a show by Eurovision Song Contest winner Conchita Wurst at the Edinburgh festival was cancelled after the support band were refused entry.

The movement of people across borders is a contentious issue around the world, with anti-immigration parties and candidates rising to prominence in places including the USA, Europe, India and Turkey. Restrictions have been toughened up on travel, even when people are visiting on holiday or are invited to perform or speak at major festivals.

"It is a global problem," said Page, adding that, in his experience, the UK and USA currently had the toughest conditions to overcome.

In the UK this anti-immigration trend is manifested by the government's "hostile environment" policies – now referred to as the "compliant environment" – which aim to create a situation where immigrants cannot access services, either public (healthcare, welfare) or private (employment, rented housing, bank accounts) unless they can prove their right to be in the country.

Critics have said the policies have meant that legal, temporary visitors – such as artists and writers – are also being punished.

Data on the exact number of artists whose applications have been rejected is hard to come by, largely because there is no specific visa for cultural visits. But cultural leaders who spoke to Index say the problem is significant.

Outright rejections can be humiliating for artists – many of whom are famous in their own countries – but festival organisers' criticisms go beyond this.

The complex and arduous process often results in delays, so even when an application eventually results in success, it is often too late for a particular event. This means many people just give up – or don't even try in the first place.

Some festivals are beginning to resist booking international artists at all.

"They don't programme them because they can't guarantee their attendance sufficiently far in advance. This effectively results in the non-programming of writers from Africa and the Middle East," said Page.

And Nelson, of Lift, said: "I was in Kampala in June and I met a lot of artists who told me, 'I'm not really fussed about the UK any more. I'm working across Africa, and if I tour in Europe, I wouldn't want to jeopardise my other European tour destinations by putting in a UK date, when the Home Office could hold up my passport indefinitely'.

"Lots of events are moving out of the UK entirely. 'Don't bother with the UK'. That's the message I'm hearing."

Paradoxically, as the challenges for staging international artists in the UK grow, so is the demand from those wanting to see them. "There is an enormous and growing appetite for these types of international events," said Hannah Trevarthen, interim director of English PEN.

And, arts leaders say, the bigger picture is that the UK is missing out on a whole school of thought. "It is not just about getting a band for a certain music festival. It is a global conversation we are cutting ourselves off from," added Nelson.

An All-Party Parliamentary Group report published in July showed that Africans were twice as likely to be rejected for visits to the UK, though cultural leaders told Index that

Lots of events are moving out of the UK entirely. 'Don't bother with the UK'. That's the message I'm hearing

CREDIT: C Brandon/Redferns/Getty

they also had particular difficulties with Middle East-based artists. Dan Gorman, director of the Shubbak festival, which celebrates art and literature from the Middle East and North Africa, says failing to provide a platform for these voices when there is such demand amounts to a freedom of expression issue.

Eman Abdelrahim, a German-based Egyptian writer, who we featured in Index recently (vol 48.2 p89), was looking forward to travelling to the UK to talk about her new short story at an event at the Liverpool Arab Arts Festival in July this year. She missed the event due to delays at the Home Office. For her, the ability to see audience reactions and understand how they interpret her writing is invaluable.

"I learn from others," she said. "When I write something, sometimes people take something completely differently from how I intended. I want to know how audiences interpret my work."

And Palestinian writer Nayrouz Qarmout was unable to attend the Edinburgh International Book Festival last year, also due to visa delays.

"Seeing me talk in person will always be so different from just reading an interview with me in a newspaper," she told Index. "With humour and body language, I try to let audiences see who I really am, so they can understand my writing from a different perspective."

Barley adds that the risk of missing out on cultural dialogue goes beyond the cultural sector, and has an impact on global trade and international relations.

In response to this story, a Home Office spokesman said: "We welcome artists and performers coming to the UK to perform, and appreciate the important contribution they make to our creative sector." The Home Office has also launched a year-long engagement process with businesses and stakeholders on a future skills-based immigration system, and is talking to the creative sector as part of that.

Barley is a proponent of a new form of "cultural passport" system which would enable trusted organisations to vouch for visitors in return for a simpler, less costly and less onerous visa application system. The organisations would stake their reputations on the fact that

WHO HAS BEEN REFUSED?

SABRY MOSBAH
Mosbah is a Tunisian folk-rock singer, songwriter and guitarist. After he was unable to secure a visa to perform at the Womad festival, his performance had to be cancelled.

WAZIMBO
Humberto Carlos Benfica, better known as Wazimbo, is a marrabenta singer from Mozambique. He was denied a visa and had to cancel his performance at Womad.

TAL NATIONAL
Several members of Niger's Tal National were denied visas, resulting in the group having to perform a stripped-down set. Tal National are ubiquitous pop stars in their home country.

EHSAN ABDOLLAHI
The Iranian illustrator was denied, then granted a visa in 2017 only after a public outcry. The following year he was named the 2018 Edinburgh Festival's artist-in-residence. However, despite this honour, his visa for that year's festival wasn't approved until just days before the event itself.
Sophia Paley

their visitors would return to their home countries, and a breach of that trust would lead to sanctions against an organisation.

If it works, it's a system that could potentially be rolled out to other UK cultural, academic and sporting organisations that arrange short-stay visits.

Many arts leaders who spoke to Index said they would welcome any simplification to the process of attaining visas for their performers, and are calling on the government to introduce simpler electronic visas for artists.

Barley said: "The result is a serious blow to this country's international reputation for openness: a justifiable assertion that we were open for business and open for tourism. Unless we can rapidly reassert that openness, the damage to the UK's reputation and business interests could be irreversible." ⊗

Charlotte Bailey is a freelance journalist

Ten tips for a safer crossing

Digital security expert **Ela Stapley** gives advice on keeping your information secure at borders

48(03): 32/34 | DOI: 10.1177/0306422019876443

TRAVELLERS ARE INCREASINGLY being asked to make personal information and social media accounts available as part of border checks, and crossing a border with electronic devices that have not been protected can leave you vulnerable if your phone or laptop is seized or you are asked to unlock it.

Below are some key steps that you can take before you travel and while at the border, to better secure your data and your devices.

Do your research

Before crossing a border, you should research the law related to technology in the places you are leaving and entering. Legislation differs from country to country and it is important to stay on top of any changes to avoid breaking the law. Keep an eye on any amendments made to media and telecommunications laws or anti-terrorism acts, which have a tendency to criminalise the use of encryption and Virtual Private Networks. Do an internet search to see if anybody has been detained or put on trial for using these tools. Travellers should also look into laws around defamation and social media and be aware of any restrictions on posting and sharing content online.

Know your adversary

If you are targeted by state bodies or organisations with sophisticated tech resources, and you are entering territory controlled by them, then you should speak to a digital security expert prior to travelling about the best way to secure your devices and your information.

Review your online profile

Your online profile is what customs guards will see if they look you up online at the border, so it is important that you know how others see you. Check for your name through all search engines, and don't look only at the general search results – review videos, images and news, too. Where possible, take steps to remove information that could put you at risk. Deleting information from the internet is difficult and a copy of that content is likely to still be available if someone should wish to find it. Changes to any information that you delete yourself will not show up on internet searches straight away.

Make a plan in case you are detained

It is important to plan what you will do and say if you are stopped or detained. Know your rights if your devices are seized or if you are asked to unlock them or hand over any passwords. If you have concerns about crossing a particular border and have the support of an employer or an organisation, speak to them about steps that can be taken in case you are detained. Ensure you have spoken to a lawyer before travelling and carry their contact details with you.

Know what information you want to protect

Review your devices for information that, if seized, could put you – or others – at risk. Look at documents and photos stored on your laptop and phone as well as information and conversations held in chat apps. Be aware that data stored in email accounts and in the cloud is at risk if your devices are seized and you have not logged out of your accounts or are asked to hand over your passwords. Review the settings of apps you use to see if they are backing up content to a cloud account linked to your devices.

CREDITS: Victor / iStock /Gary Waters/Ikon

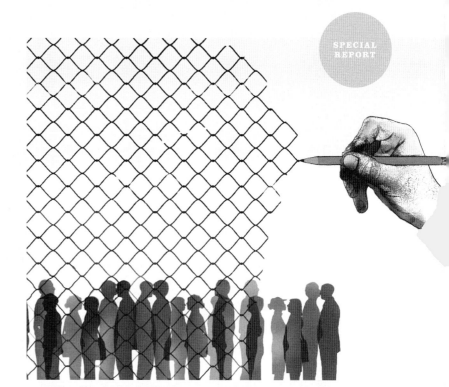

Create a secure way to back up and store information

Once you have identified what information you need to keep, you should create a secure back-up of this content before travelling. It is a good idea to back up the information to an external hard drive, which you should then encrypt and store in a secure place. You should get into the habit of backing up information from your devices regularly.

Think about your devices

If you are travelling with data that you do not want others to access, you should either securely remove this information from the devices before travelling or buy new devices. These new devices should hold only non-sensitive information and you should not link them to any accounts that you would not want others to access. You may want to carry out factory resets of your devices, which restore them to their original settings, before each border crossing. This will permanently delete all content and apps that are on them, so ensure you back up any information first.

If there is a high probability that your devices will be seized then you may want to consider setting them to remote-wipe. This means that content from your phone and laptop will erase automatically if instructed to do so. Unless you have created a back-up you will lose all data on them. Remote-wipe must be set up in advance and you will need a person you trust to access your account and initiate the wipe. Your devices will wipe only if they are connected to mobile data or WiFi.

Preparing your laptop

Make sure your computer is password-protected and the operating system is up to date. Review the device to ensure all sensitive documentation is removed and backed up and that the laptop has been securely wiped. Log out of all your accounts and apps and clear your browsing →

WHAT DOES THE FUTURE HOLD?

Protecting your information while crossing borders may become more complicated in the future as governments roll out new technology at airports and customs officials are given more powers. Below are some developments to watch out for.

MORE FACIAL RECOGNITION

While facial recognition technology is already being used by security in some airports to confirm the identity of passport holders, airline companies and airports are starting to use it as a way to check in and to board planes. This raises concerns about which companies are storing your data and who else has access to it.

INCREASED LEVELS OF ONLINE SCRUTINY FOR VISA APPLICANTS

Governments could possibly follow the US model of asking for a person's social media handle as part of the process of applying for a visa. Earlier this year, the US government started asking certain visa applicants to supply all social media user-names and made it a criminal offence not to do so.

TIGHTENED GOVERNMENT CONTROLS RESTRICTING ONLINE PRIVACY

Changes to legislation by governments around the world are making it increasingly difficult to cross borders with encrypted devices or with tools that allow you to circumnavigate online censorship. This makes it easier to detain, arrest and charge people as well as limiting access to the internet once inside the country.

→ history from each search engine. This will stop border guards being able to access your accounts without your password. If the law permits it, you should encrypt your laptop to protect content on the device being looked at without your knowledge.

Preparing your phone

Create a long pin lock for your phone and update it to the latest version of the operating system as this patches any known bugs. Review your phone to ensure there is no sensitive data on it, back up the content and carry out a factory reset. If you install apps after the factory reset then download only the ones you need for your trip. Log out and uninstall any apps that give away personal information, such as social media apps. You will need to go into the settings section of the phone to do this rather than removing them from the home screen – you can install them again once you have crossed the border. Review your contacts and remove any that are sensitive – you will

need to remove them from both the device and the cloud account. Finally, you should go into the settings section of your phone and clear your cache. This will delete your browsing history.

What to watch for at the border

You should turn off all devices before you cross the border as this will enable full-disk encryption, if it has been set up. This means that a border guard will have to ask you for the password in order to read the content on your device. Keep an eye on your devices at all times and watch to see if anyone tampers with them. If a device is taken away and later given back to you, be aware that the content of that device could have been copied and that malware, including spyware, could have been installed. ⊗

Ela Stapley trains journalists around the world in digital security

CROSSWORD ANSWERS

Everything you add to the truth subtracts from the truth (Solzhenitsyn)

Across

1 ethnic (ETHIC round N)
5 remarque ((no defn) homophone of remark)
9 veer (anag of EVER)
10 abstractor (ABS + TRACTOR)
11 arranged (ARRAN + G(r)E(e)D)
12 instep (IN + STEP)
13 atmospherics (anag of HARPISTCOMES)
17 solzhenitsyn ((no defn) Z inside anag of SINHONESTLY)
20 miller ((no defn) M + ILLER)
22 gordimer ((no defn) DIM inside GORER)
24 stampeding (STING round AMPED)
25 grey ((mea)GREY(am))
26 infrared (RAREFIND)
27 expose (EX + POSE)

Down

2 the truth (THET(a) + RUTH)
3 narrators (anag of RANTROAR + S)
4 chang ((no defn) HANG after C)
5 rushdie ((no defn) RUSH + DIE)
6 mortician (cryptic defn)
7 rocks (double defn)
8 unowed (UNO + WED)
14 polar bear (anag of ORPARABLE)
15 sitting up (UP after SITTING)
16 pyrenees (PYRE + SEEN upwards)
18 hog-tied (HOG + TIED)
19 milton ((no defn) TON after MIL)
21 lamer (LA MER)
23 rogue ((b)ROGUE)

Export laws

China's big tech companies are selling their surveillance to the world, **Ryan Gallagher** reports

48(03): 35/37 I DOI: 10.1177/0306422019876445

UNDER THE RULE of President Xi Jinping, the internet crackdown in China has intensified in recent years. President Xi has recognised that through aggressively censoring and monitoring the internet, he can suppress dissent and manipulate public opinion. But he also views China's internet model as a tool through which he can export his government's influence worldwide, both ideologically and economically.

In April 2018, President Xi gave a speech in Beijing at the National Cybersecurity and Informatisation Work Conference, where he stated that he wanted his government to "move forward the construction of China as a cyber superpower through indigenous innovation".

As such, China is now spreading its model of the internet as one aspect of its Belt and Road Initiative, a development strategy focused on infrastructure projects that enhance Chinese trade and influence.

According to the US NGO Freedom House, Chinese companies are increasingly exporting surveillance and censorship technologies to other authoritarian governments, including those in Bahrain, Belarus, Cuba, Egypt, Ethiopia, Iran, Kazakhstan, Burma, Russia, Saudi Arabia, Sudan, Syria, Thailand, the United Arab Emirates, Uzbekistan, Venezuela, and Vietnam.

"Democracy is on the retreat and the idea of an open, global, uncensored internet is under attack," said Adrian Shahbaz, research director for technology and democracy at NGO Freedom House. "Other countries are moving towards the so-called 'China Model' because governments are viewing it as advantageous in terms of enforcing their own ideas of state sovereignty on the internet."

Chinese companies providing surveillance or censorship equipment to governments include Sinovatio, Vixtel, Hisilicon, Longhope, Semptian, Yitu, Hikvision, and CloudWalk. Guangzhou-based CloudWalk is currently working with the government in Zimbabwe to build a national facial recognition database and monitoring system in cities throughout the country.

China has long cultivated close relations with Zimbabwe and has invested billions in building the African nation's infrastructure and exploiting its diamond and platinum mines. But the CloudWalk deal represented a new frontier for China: it is believed that this is the first time that a Chinese company has entered Africa with an Artificial Intelligence surveillance technology.

Under the deal it has signed with the Zimbabwean government, CloudWalk will gain access to photographs of millions of Zimbabwean citizens. According to Chinese state media reports, CloudWalk plans to use the photographs to train its systems to better recognise faces with darker skin. This will improve the accuracy of China's facial recognition and artificial intelligence systems, giving the country's companies an edge against competitors in Europe and North America.

Arthur Gwagwa, a senior research associate at Kenya's Strathmore University, believes China is treating developing countries as "laboratories" to improve its surveillance technologies. "For a long time China has been coming here and working on infrastructure," said Gwanga. "But that has changed. Now artificial intelligence is the new currency for development, for geopolitics, for world dominance."

Now artificial intelligence is the new currency for development, for geopolitics, for world dominance

CREDIT: Matt Kenyon/Ikon

→ The provision of the facial recognition system to Zimbabwe raises human rights concerns, given that the African nation's security agencies have a long record of targeting activists and critics. It is highly likely, Gwagwa says, that the Chinese technology will be used to monitor protests and track opponents of the ruling regime. "We see facial recognition being used now at political rallies, with drones to take photos," he said. "The primary motive is social control."

In other African nations, China has entered into similar deals. In Kenya, Chinese technology giant Huawei has set up a new communications network that connects thousands of surveillance cameras to police departments across the country. In Angola, a Chinese company has provided the government with technology that is reportedly intended to record biometric information about citizens, such as fingerprints and facial images. And in Ethiopia, the Chinese telecommunications company ZTE has provided the government with surveillance technology that monitors internet activity and phone calls, according to Human Rights Watch.

Many of the systems that are exported from China to other parts of the world are designed or developed in the southern city of Shenzhen. In the Nanshan district of the city, a thriving technology centre, the likes of Huawei and ZTE have large offices. But there are other companies in the area whose names are not as well known to the public – because the work that they carry out is secret.

On the eighth floor of a massive office block in Shenzhen's High-Tech South Zone, Semptian has its headquarters. Semptian is among the growing new breed of Chinese technology companies specialising in surveillance and censorship equipment, which it manufactures and sells to governments.

Earlier this year, as part of an undercover investigation, I approached Semptian posing as a potential customer. According to documents which I saw, and a video produced by the company, they are marketing a surveillance system which can be covertly placed within phone and internet networks to monitor people's emails, phone calls, text messages, mobile phone locations, and web browsing activity.

The surveillance system, named Aegis, was designed to monitor the private communications of entire populations of people

The system, named Aegis, was designed to monitor the private communications of entire populations. A document that details the system's capabilities stated that it could be used to track "location information for everyone in the country," "show the connections of everyone," and also "block certain information [on the] internet from being visited".

The system which according to a Semptian employee, is already used in China to monitor 200 million Chinese, has also been sold to other countries, including to authoritarian regimes in the Middle East and North Africa.

Semptian offered, via emails, to provide an Aegis installation with the capacity to monitor the internet activity of five million people for a cost of between $1.5 million and $2.5 million. The only countries the company said it would not deal with would be Iran and Syria – everywhere else, including North Korea, Saudi Arabia, Belarus or Sudan, where authorities have a record of detaining and torturing their critics – it apparently viewed as potential clients. Semptian did not respond to a request for a comment on this story.

Semptian's effort to sell its surveillance and censorship equipment globally is emblematic of the Chinese government's strategy to export its technological and ideological framework over its own borders. It appears likely that, as China's influence on the global stage continues to grow, so too will its authoritarian version of the internet. ⊗

Ryan Gallagher is an investigative journalist for The Intercept

At the world's toughest border

South Koreans who try and get in touch with their North Korean family can face prison for making contact, **Steven Borowiec** reports

48(03): 38/39 I DOI: 10.1177/0306422019876449

EVERY THURSDAY AFTERNOON, activists gather outside the gates of an ancient park in downtown Seoul to speak out about North Korea, knowing that what they say could land them in jail. The purpose of the weekly gathering is to call for the release of prisoners who were sentenced for violating the National Security Law – legislation dating back to 1948 that criminalises speech deemed supportive of North Korea and unapproved communication with anyone in the North.

While in South Korea there is near constant chatter about how relations with North Korea's government are improving, when it comes to South Koreans' ability to communicate across the border, the old strictures remain in place.

But pressure on the government of President Moon Jae-in is growing.

Later this year, Minbyun – Lawyers for a Democratic Society, one of South Korea's most prominent civic groups, plans to organise a series of lectures and cultural events across South Korea under the title, I'm a victim of the National Security Law, where people who have been jailed or harassed by the government for their comments on North Korea speak publicly about their experiences.

Chae Hee-joon, a lawyer from Minbyun, told Index: "Under the [President] Moon Jae-in government, the number of cases of people being penalised for violations of the National Security Law has decreased, but the law's chilling effect on people's freedoms of thought, consciousness and expression has remained the same."

The law first came into effect when the Korean peninsula was on the brink of war. Under the law, people have gone to prison for actions as simple as owning North Korean literature or speaking favourably of the North's ruling dynasty.

Kwon Oh-huen, a slight, softly-spoken man in his 70s, has been coming to the Thursday protest meetings in central Seoul for decades. He takes the microphone to call for the release of 12 prisoners currently serving time for the crime of praising North Korea. Kwon and other opponents of the law argue that the law uses too vague a definition of what constitutes "praise", and that it is an unjust infringement on freedom of expression.

"Our government must guarantee freedom of conscience," Kwon told Index. "If we lock up even one person for their beliefs, that means our society is barbaric."

The 250-kilometre border that separates north and south has only one active crossing, which is heavily guarded by the military on both sides. Tall barbed wire fences run along the border everywhere else.

If a South Korean citizen wishes to send a letter or make a phone call to someone in North Korea, they first must seek permission from their government. If a South Korean national happens to meet a North Korean citizen while travelling overseas they are required to report that activity back to their government immediately. Failure to take these steps can lead to charges of having violated the National Security Law.

> *If a South Korean citizen wishes to send a letter or make a phone call to someone in North Korea, they first must seek permission from their government*

CREDIT: Ed Jones/AFP/Getty

The ostensible purpose of these controls is to prevent infiltration of North Korean spies into South Korea, and to prevent South Korean nationals from acting as aides or informants to those spies.

Kwon has direct experience with the law. In 2014, his home was raided and he was investigated after he said at one of the weekly protests that the late North Korean dictator, Kim Jong-il, was someone who performed "good deeds" for the Korean people. It wasn't his first brush with the law. In the early 1970s, he spent three and a half years in prison for taking part in violent rallies against the military dictatorship that ran South Korea at the time.

Born in 1937, in a mountainous province south of Seoul, Kwon's parents died when he was in his teens, and he moved to the capital. He found companionship in the city's community of left-wing activists who resisted the US-allied South Korean government of the time, and longed for unification with the North.

When he is not being called a "commie" and a pro-North Korea stooge in the South Korean media, Kwon is sometimes called a "lifelong youth" for remaining dedicated to activism into his old age.

Beyond seeking changes to particular laws, Kwon sees his mission as spreading understanding. "Koreans in the south and north don't really have different ideologies. We're all one people: it's politics that divides us. If we were able to talk directly and share information we could come to understand each other better."

Most South Koreans with family in the north have, over the decades of division, lost contact with their relatives. For defectors who now live in the south, there are the impediments of South Korean law to overcome as well as North Korea's own strict controls.

"The reality is that, for the majority of North Koreans who leave for places like South Korea, the UK and Japan, contact with family they leave behind is costly, unreliable, and sporadic," said Markus Bell, a lecturer in Korean and Japanese Studies at the University of Sheffield.

Those who can afford it seek help in the black market of merchants and fixers who do business in and around North Korea. "Many of the North Koreans I worked with in Japan and in South Korea were able to speak with, and send money to, their families through informal, illegal networks of middlemen, working in the borderlands of places like Yanji, China," Bell said.

North Korean-born poet Lee Ka-yeon tackles this inability to keep in touch in her award-winning 2015 collection "Waiting for Mom". Lee says that when she fled North Korea in 2010, she did so without informing anyone, even her immediate family, because of the fear that word of her plan would get around and she could be arrested before departing. She now lives in Seoul and says she has had no contact with her family in the years since.

Unlike some North Korean-born writers, her work does not feature shrill criticism of the regime. Instead, her writing mulls over the emotional pain of separation from loved ones.

"I don't even know if my mom is still alive," Lee said in an interview. "I wish I could just ask her simple things, like how her health is, if she's eating well."

Kwon says he hopes the division of the Koreas won't last and that the South Korean government will ease limitations on interaction between South and North Koreans, paving the way for eventual reunification.

"To really achieve peace, we have to be able to communicate," he said. ⊗

Steven Borowiec is a freelance writer based in Seoul, South Korea

ABOVE: A military fence separates a young South Korean girl from North Korea as she gazes into the distance at Imjingak park, south of the Military Demarcation Line and Demilitarised Zone (DMZ). South Korean families divided during the Korean War visit the DMZ to pray for their relatives in the North, most often on the occasion of the Lunar New Year

Rowson

48(03): 40/41 | DOI: 10.1177/0306422019876450

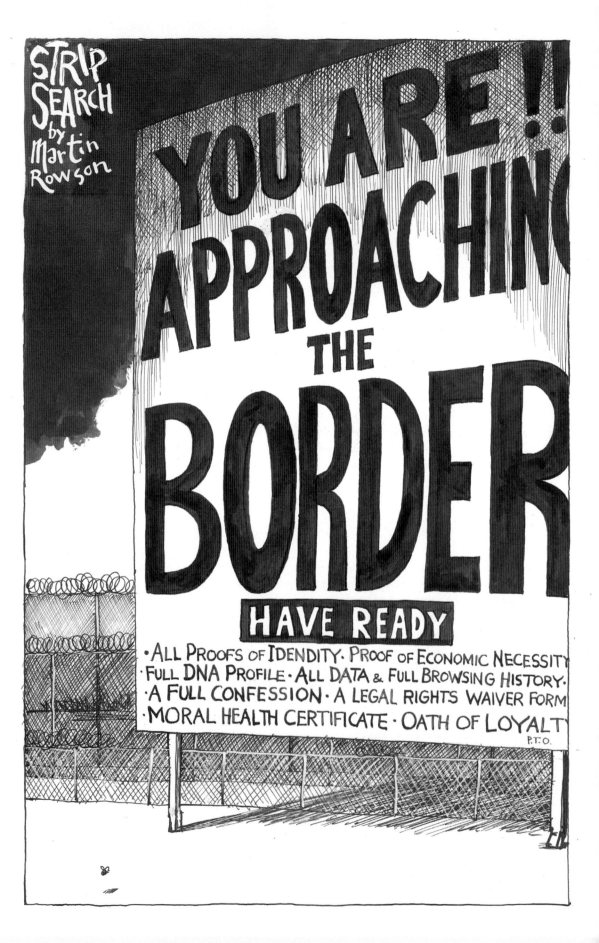

MARTIN ROWSON is a cartoonist for The Guardian and the author of various books, including The Communist Manifesto (2018), a graphic novel adaption of the famous 19th century book

Inside the silent zone

Analysts believe the situation in Western Sahara may soon escalate but, as **Silvia Nortes** writes, there are no journalists there to report either side of an impending conflict

48(03): 42/43 | DOI: 10.1177/0306422019876451

SALAMU HAMUDI ARRIVED in Spain from the refugee camp where he was born thanks to the Vacaciones en Paz (or Holidays for Peace) project, which sends Saharawi children – those from Western Sahara – for holidays with Spanish families.

Today, Hamudi works as a freelance journalist based in Spain and is part of the Sahara Press League, which integrates Saharawi journalists based in Europe to allow them to "be ambassadors of a conflict we want to be known", as Hamudi told Index.

There is very little known about what is happening in Western Sahara, which is a disputed area mainly controlled by Morocco and bordering Algeria and Mauritania. A report that came out this year from the Spanish branch of Reporters Sans Frontières, called Western Sahara: A Desert for Journalists, warned about the information-drought in the territory.

"There are no independent media nor Saharawi journalists recognised as such by the Moroccan authorities," the report said.

Thus, the struggle for the establishment of borders and the control of the territory has resulted in the absence of freedom of expression and the press. "Morocco does not want to talk about Western Sahara, and every time a

Moroccan journalist tries to report on it, he is dismissed and prosecuted for attacking national integrity," Alfonso Armada, president of RSF Spain, told Index. "In addition to the artificially drawn geographical borders, a border of silence has been established."

The instability of Western Sahara dates back to 1976, when Spain left the area after more than a century of colonisation. After Spain's withdrawal, it was initially split between Morocco and Mauritania. In 1979, Mauritania withdrew, abandoning its claim, but Morocco immediately claimed the whole territory. Today, it is divided between areas controlled by Morocco and those controlled by the Polisario Front, the national liberation movement wanting independence for the Saharawi people. As of December 2017, nearly 175,000 Saharawi refugees were living in camps in Tindouf, Algeria, according to figures from UNHCR, the UN Refugee Agency.

In addition, Western Sahara is divided by an earth wall, called the Berm, with barbed wire fences and guards. At 2,700km, it is one the largest walls in the world and was built by Morocco during the 1980s to contain the Polisario.

The area now exists in a kind of stalemate policed by the United Nations. During Morocco's King Mohammed VI's 20-year reign, four UN special representatives for the Sahara have resigned without resolving the conflict, despite the fact that the UN defends the right to self-determination in Western Sahara.

That's why, according to recent reports in the Wall Street Journal, US President Donald Trump's security adviser, John Bolton, has condemned the UN's lack of success and thrown his weight behind a "contentious" plan "turning the screws on the UN and trying to force the rival parties to cut a deal". That deal, according to the WSJ, is unlikely to include a new independent country of Western Sahara. Either way, if UN troops withdraw there could be conflict in a region which has recently been relatively stable.

But because of a complete lack of freedom of the press, there is very little discussion of the situation or reporting from either side. Hamudi feels ashamed that "the situation of the press in

BELOW: A map showing part of north Africa, including Morocco and Western Sahara

CREDIT: (left) Chris Peccoraro/iStock; (right) Henryk Sadura/Picfair

Western Sahara is not under scrutiny as it is in Turkey, Venezuela or Saudi Arabia". He added: "There is no freedom of expression. One cannot practise journalism. [It's] not only Sahrawi journalists: foreign correspondents are returned to their country, and Morocco does not even allow international observers in."

Indeed, journalism in Western Sahara is closely monitored by Moroccan authorities who, as Freedom House reflects, "ensure that reporting does not dispute Morocco's sovereignty over Western Sahara".

As RSF says, there are numerous cases of repression exerted by Morocco on the press – torture, detentions, persecutions, harassment, slander, technological sabotage and long jail terms.

Reporters El Bachir Khadda, Hassan Dah, Abdellahi Lakhfawni and Mohamed Lamin Haddi were arrested in 2010 while covering the Gdeim Izik protest camp in Western Sahara's Southern Province. They are still in prison and are being prosecuted for crimes including allegations that they belonged to an armed group and caused the death of Moroccan officers through violence. The crimes they are alleged to have committed carry sentences of between 20 years and life imprisonment.

In June 2014, Mahmoud El Haissan, a television correspondent for RASD, which is based in the Tindouf refugee camps in Algeria, filmed a confrontation between pro-independence demonstrators and Moroccan security forces in Laayoune. El Haissan was later arrested at home and taken to Laayoune's Cárcel Negra (black prison) for "belonging to an armed group, obstruction of public roads, attacks on officials in the exercise of their duties and destruction of public property". He was sentenced to 18 months in jail and suffered physical abuse.

Foreign journalists are not free to report. In fact, as Armada highlights, foreign correspondents were expelled nine years ago, and "information on Western Sahara is very sporadic".

In June this year, Spanish photojournalist Judith Prat was expelled from the Western Saharan city of Laayoune two hours after arriving in the city. In February, Spanish journalist

The struggle for the establishment of borders and the control of the territory has resulted in the absence of freedom of expression and the press

Ana Cortés and her Italian colleague, Giovanni Cortceli, who were attempting to report from the border area, were arrested by Moroccan authorities, interrogated, assaulted and finally deported.

The only people still reporting from the area is Equipe Media, a group of journalists and activists set up in 2009 to break the information blockade imposed by Morocco. In order to do their job safely, Equipe Media journalists have to resort to clandestine meetings. "Laayoune is taken militarily. No journalist can access Western Sahara – we are targets for Moroccan police forces," said Mayara. "We manage to hold our meetings in secret places or in the countryside. We also get in touch secretly with the organisers of demonstrations to know where they will take place and send our cameramen to roofs in the area so that they can film."

No matter what, journalism proudly does its best to survive. "We are working under such conditions that we could say a new way of doing journalism has been born in Western Sahara," said Mayara. "We understand it is hard, but we will continue reporting despite risks and threats." ⊗

ABOVE: A mosque in Dakhla, Western Sahara

***Silvia Nortes** is a freelance journalist based in Spain*

The great news wall of China

Karoline Kan looks at how the Chinese government keeps news from getting across its borders, so it can control what its citizens know

48(03): 44/46 | DOI: 10.1177/0306422019876453

IT WAS NOT until three weeks after the Hong Kong protests started that 28-year-old Chen Minmin began hearing about it. However, Chen does not care how the protests began or what they are for. News available in mainland China never elaborated on that. Instead, the first thing she heard was from China's state-owned Xinhua news agency, calling the protesters "extremists" who undermined the rule of law in Hong Kong and harm Hong Kong's interests by violence.

The way China handles information about the protests in Hong Kong is just the latest example of how the government works to keep news coverage it doesn't like from filtering across the border. The border between the Chinese mainland and Hong Kong is like a solid wall separating two communities ruled by different laws, in different political systems.

Chen works in an IT company in Shenzhen, a city 28 kilometres away from Hong Kong. Despite living so close, Chen knew nothing about the first few weeks of peaceful protests, thanks to China's powerful blanket censorship machine. However, since the protests on 1 July, when a group smashed through government headquarters and occupied the Legislative Council, information suddenly flooded through on Chen's social media.

Chinese state media has issued pictures and videos about the protests, referring to "riots", "mobs" and "criminal acts of violence". Information about why Hong Kong's residents were protesting is left out, and the media and China's foreign ministry calls out "foreign hands" behind the protest. Such one-sided and sometimes twisted information is used by the Chinese government to create fear of violence and foreign intervention and to stress the importance of stability – which, in the government's narrative, can be achieved only through the current Chinese political system and by Chinese Communist Party rule.

Under the basic law, which ensures the principle of "one country, two systems", Hong Kong currently has an independent legislative and judicial system, and a large measure of freedom of speech. The protesters worry about all this being eroded, and they first began to demonstrate after the introduction of a bill that would have meant Hong Kong residents could be extradited to the mainland for specific crimes. The city is currently also a popular destination for migrants and dissidents from the mainland who flee political turbulence and persecution. On the Chinese side of the border, activists are monitored and threatened, most protests are banned, freedom of speech is on paper only, and the judicial system is invoked to resist "harmful Western influences".

What's as powerful and efficient as a physical border is the internet wall China has set up. The great firewall, which is officially called the golden shield project, censors the internet and blocks websites that have content critical of the Chinese government and the party. The government hires censors to delete "harmful" content

> *Such one-sided and sometimes twisted information is used by the Chinese government to create fear of violence and foreign intervention*

CREDITS: IStock

and post pro-government comments. Internet companies also delete content on their platforms because they are afraid of being punished by the authorities. China is also trying to control information abroad. Facebook and Twitter said they had taken down thousands of posts and suspended accounts they believed were part of a Chinese government campaign to "sow political discord" in Hong Kong. YouTube also announced in August that it had disabled 210 channels which were seeking to spread disinformation about the protesters there.

The Chinese government does all this,

because censorship and manipulation of information work. When I asked Chen what she thought of the Hong Kong protests, she said: "No matter what excuses the protesters in Hong Kong have, their final goal is to make a mess in Hong Kong and put China in a difficult situation." Most mainlanders who I know agree with Chen. "You see how censorship and the way state media chooses to present the story is shaping people's opinions in China," said James Griffiths, author of the book The Great Firewall of China. "If the only information about the Hong Kong protests

China has created an information bubble in which truth is not always about what happened but about what everyone in the bubble believes happened

→ you have access to are pictures of how the legislative building got smashed up, or occasional pictures of police with a bloody nose, it would massively reshape how you perceive the information and how you think of the protest."

What's worse is that although traditionally censorship worked in a top-down way, technological advances mean the government is now able to set up systems to monitor people's speech and behaviour to force self-censorship. There are surveillance cameras in the streets of most Chinese major cities, and facial recognition can locate any individual within a few seconds. In the north-west region of Xinjiang, the police forced ethnic minorities, mainly Uighurs, to install spy apps on their smartphones to detect "irregularities or deviations" from what the police considered normal, all in the name of fighting terrorism and separatism.

China even plans to build a nationwide reputation-ranking system, known as the social credit system, for its citizens and businesses, using big data analysis. People worry the system would be used to silence dissidents.

The social credit system might take a while to function well, but its effect is already apparent. A journalist friend who is working in Hong Kong told me she didn't post anything on social media about the protest during the first three weeks when China blocked the information. She is sure her social media is monitored and she is worried her behaviour could bring pressure on her family in the mainland.

She is probably not paranoid. Earlier this year, a few hours after I text-chatted with another friend working for a Western news organisation about an unsuccessful economic development zone in my hometown, police knocked on my parents' door, saying I had posted "improper comments online". I was travelling, so the police harassed my parents as a way of giving me a warning.

What my friend and I were talking about made headlines in international newspapers a few years ago because of a chemical blast. Our conversation had nothing to do with the blast, or anything political, but we had alerted the police simply by mentioning the place's name.

On the 30th anniversary of the Tiananmen Square protests this June, while the anniversary was on front-pages all around the world outside China, inside the country nothing happened and nobody risked talking about it in public. Many Chinese people who were born after 1989 have never heard of it.

With the help of the great firewall, China patrols its own borders, using its own internet, on which people discuss China's own priorities, and it sets the narrative on international affairs. China has created an information bubble in which truth is not always about what happened but about what everyone in the bubble believes happened.

In 27 years, the basic law that guarantees Hong Kong's freedom will expire and it could mean the both the border wall and the information wall will be expanded there. However, it might not take even that long for China to stretch its hands across the border. Chinese government mouthpieces are already openly accusing Hong Kong media that are free from censorship of being the troublemakers in this year's protests, and calling the media "the schemer, organiser, and participant of violence".

As the conflicts escalate between police and the protesters, China also escalates the words it uses: from "mobs" to "separatists", and even "signs of terrorism". Nobody knows what the next term it uses will be, but it is heading in a disturbing direction. What's more worrying is there might be hundreds of millions of people in mainland China cheering for that result. ⊗

Karoline Kan is a regular contributor to Index, based in Beijing. She is author of Under Red Skies, her autobiography

Kenya: who is watching you?

Wana Udobang speaks to a Kenyan journalist who worries about her government's ability to know every detail about her

48(03): 47/47 | DOI: 10.1177/0306422019876454

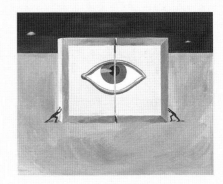

CREDIT: Gary Bates/Ikon

" **I HATE THE IDEA** of somebody watching me everywhere I go. Imagine meeting a news source in a hotel and you don't know that you have already been marked. How the hell do I get my info?" said journalist Catherine Gicheru.

"Even a simple engagement between me and somebody else – politicians can use that to make you a victim, too."

Gicheru, country manager at Code for Africa – a technology and data journalism initiative – was talking to Index about concerns relating to the new biometric testing programme being introduced by the Kenyan government using a French company.

The tests are mandatory, and data being gathered includes GPS co-ordinates for home addresses, fingerprints, retina and iris scans and voice samples. Around 21 million Kenyans have reportedly already registered with the system, which was part of a $59 million project led by Idemia, a French multinational company specialising in security and identity management.

However, this company has run into problems and the Kenyan national assembly has now voted to suspend it from government contracts for 10 years after an alleged violation of the Companies Act.

Whatever the reason a government gives for collecting data on its citizens, people will always be wary about how it is collected, how it is stored, and its possible uses, Gicheru told Index.

"We live in a country where the more information the government has about us, the more power they have to use against [us]," she said.

"For me, as a journalist, it should not happen … until we put in place the securities and the laws to ensure that my information is secure and protected."

The biggest concern of many media workers is the possible surveillance of journalists investigating institutional corruption and abuse of power. How do journalists protect sources, whistleblowers and themselves?

She believes it is too much power to give to a government which has not previously acted in the interest of its citizens. The security of other forms of personal information had already proved to be a problem, so she is concerned about what could happen with the biometric data and what kind of security has been put in place to keep it safe.

"We shouldn't cede to government at all – especially without any kind of protection," she said. Gicheru is insistent on the need for a public conversation around the use and ownership of private citizens' information and thinks the Kenyan government needs to be willing to bring in proper data protection measures.

"Technology needs to serve the people, not the people [serve] the technology." ⊗

Wana Udobang is a freelance journalist, based in Nigeria

Top ten states closing their doors to ideas

National borders are getting scarier, and blocking the flow of information. But which are the toughest in the globe? **Mark Frary** reports

48(03): 48/49 I DOI: 10.1177/0306422019876439

IN THE PAST century and a half, technologies from the telegraph to the internet have threatened to make physical borders irrelevant. But authoritarian regimes continue to find ways to stop information passing in or out of their territories. This article looks at the 10 countries (listed alphabetically) whose borders represent the toughest barriers to the flow of ideas today.

China
China hit rock bottom in Freedom House's Freedom on the Net report 2018, which called it "the worst abuser of internet freedom". The country has also tries to export its surveillance technology to others. Bach Avezdjanov, programme officer at Columbia Global Freedom of Expression, said: "With the Chinese great firewall, it is effective because not as many people there speak English. Physical borders create barriers of language and culture and that gets ingrained unless people are exposed to something else. "With China, everyone says why don't people use VPNs? The thing is, even people who have heard of them don't really know how to set them up properly." In spring 2019, the country began blocking all language versions of the Wikipedia site.

Eritrea
Eritrea has one of the world's lowest internet penetration rates, just 1.3% of the country's five million strong population. This is part of the government's control of access to information. The country has repeatedly been ranked worst in the world for press freedom by Reporters Without Borders (RSF) and there have been no independent sources of media within the country since a 2001 crackdown. Many people get their news about the country through the Eritrean Press page on Facebook, which is edited anonymously from Britain.

India
India leads the world when it comes to blocking the flow of information using internet shutdowns although it does have a vibrant media. According to advocacy group Access Now's 2018 #Keepiton Report, India represented two thirds of all shutdowns recorded. Kashmir is the focus of the overwhelming majority of these shutdowns – representing more than half of those recorded since 2012, before being completed locked down this summer after Prime Minister Modi's decision to take away its autonomous region status.

Iran
Protests in Iran in 2017 and 2018 saw a clampdown on social media and the internet by the government. In January 2017, administrators of groups of more than 5,000 people on the messaging app Telegram were forced to started registering with the authorities in Iran. A number of administrators were arrested ahead of elections in May 2017. Freedom House ranked the country second last, just ahead of China, in its 2018 Freedom on the Net report. Iran strictly controls journalists' entry to the country.

Kazakhstan
Jillian York, director for international freedom of expression at the Electronic Frontier Foundation, says Kazakhstan should be highlighted for its "extensive surveillance network". Kazakhstan's borders to the outside world have grown even tougher since Nursultan Nazarbayev took over after the collapse of the Soviet Union in

CREDIT: iStock

1990. In 2018, internet users in the country began to notice that for a couple of hours each evening, websites such as Facebook and YouTube were difficult, or impossible, to reach. This throttling of the internet was in response to exiled opposition leader Mukhtar Ablyazov live-streaming his criticism of the government. Nazarbayev resigned in March 2019, but that has not stopped the shutdowns.

Mexico

"It is very difficult to get ideas out of Mexico," said Bertin Leblanc, editor-in-chief of Reporters Without Borders. According to the International Federation of Journalists, 11 people in the media were killed in 2018 and this grim record looks set to be broken in 2019. On 11 June 2019, crime reporter Norma Sarabia was killed in Huimanguillo, the seventh journalist to be killed so far in 2019 and the 149th to die since 2000, according to the Mexican human rights commission. In this murderous climate, it is no surprise investigative journalism is under threat.

North Korea

The presence of Kim Jong-Un's totalitarian state on this list is inevitable. It's difficult for international visitors, especially journalists, to enter. The Korean Central News Agency is the only official source of news for the country's media, and North Koreans who consume other media can be sent to concentration camps. Only senior officials and foreigners may access the internet. North Koreans can only access the strictly controlled Kwangmyong intranet. The Flash Drives for Freedom campaign smuggles information across the border on USB sticks, saying these had reached 1.3 million North Koreans by the end of 2018.

Pakistan

Coming second to India in terms of internet shutdowns is Pakistan, Access Now reported there were at least 12 shutdowns in 2018. There were also two shutdowns of the mobile phone and text message networks last year. The Open Observatory of Network Interference, which carries out real-time analysis of

the internet to detect network anomalies and censorship, says that "multiple tests conducted in Pakistan show that 'middle boxes' (software which could potentially be used for censorship and/or traffic manipulation) [are] present in Pakistani networks".

Russia

Russia continues to restrict information flowing in and out of the country. Avezdjanov at Columbia Global Freedom of Expression, said: "In Russia, a lot of censorship is trying to target messenging apps as this is where a lot of political discourse has moved to – away from websites." In 2017, Russia banned virtual private networks, encrypted connections to the internet that can help people to access the internet freely. While the law does not seem to have been enforced widely, in early 2019 the federal censor, Roskomnadzor, stepped up action against VPNs by demanding that leading providers connected their servers to its network. The messaging app Telegram was blocked in April 2018 for failing to provide the security services with users' encryption keys.

Yemen

Yemen is dangerous for journalists. Nine people working in the media died in 2018 and journalists are abducted or detained, never to be seen again. In 2015, journalist and human rights activist Abdel Karim al-Khaiwani was gunned down outside his house. Those responsible have never been found. The government is also fond of throttling the internet and shutting down social media networks. A RSF report said: "In all parts of the country, citizen-journalists are monitored and can be arrested for a single social network post." Veteran Yemeni correspondent Laura Silvia Battaglia said: "Journalists are often stopped by militias at borders and everywhere, searched, and detained." ⊗

Mark Frary is a journalist and author. He wrote De/Cipher, a guide to cryptography

PICTURED: Graffiti
depicting an eye acts
as a window between
the east and west
sides of the Berlin
Wall, 1989

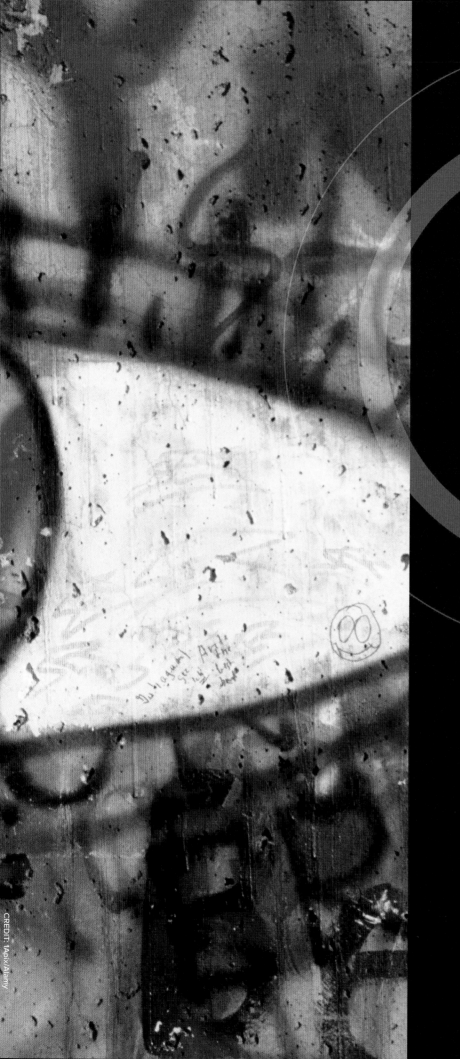

CREDIT: 1Apix/Alamy

IN FOCUS

Germany's surveillance fears

Thirty years after the fall of the Berlin wall and the disbanding of East Germany's secret police, the Stasi, Germans are worried about who is watching them. **Cathrin Schaer** reports

48(03): 52/53 | DOI: 10.1177/0306422019875092

THIS AUTUMN, THE German government will decide whether a proposal to allow state security services to plant spyware on private citizens' computers and phones should go ahead. This would allow them to spy on any citizens they suspected of wrong-doing.

It is all part of interior minister Horst Seehofer's draft law on the "modernisation of the Office for the Protection of the Constitution". This office, one of several German security agencies, has only minimal power to enforce laws and is mostly charged with keeping a close eye on would-be terrorists inside the country.

The proposal caused an immediate outcry. Internet privacy advocates called it a "licence to hack". Journalists saw it as an attack on press freedom, saying they wouldn't be able to protect sources. And parents worried that security services would be watching their children after Seehofer said that even under-14s could have been radicalised by extremist groups.

In East Germany, the communist government would often put cameras or listening devices in homes without citizens knowing and, as Konstantin von Notz, current deputy leader of the Green party in the German parliament, pointed out, these new plans would "endanger the fundamental rights of millions of people and the digital economy. Instead of a million more bugs in our apartments we need more secure devices and more clearly defined legal standards [for them]."

This year marks 30 years since the fall of the Berlin Wall and the end of the East German government and its secret police, better known as the Stasi (short for *Staatssicherheitsdienst*, or state security service).

East Germany was well known as one of the most surveilled nations in the world, and when the government dissolved in 1989, the ministry for state security had 91,000 employees and a further estimated 100,000 informers on its books. These informers were known as "unofficial employees", and at their peak they made up almost 1% of the East German population. They were everywhere, all the time – children spied on parents, sports coaches on athletes and teachers on students.

There is no doubt that almost 40 years of this level of surveillance and the constant need for self-censorship has had an enormous impact on German policy in this area. History has taught Germans the price of privacy.

"Some online platforms know more about us than the Stasi knew about their citizens," Iyad Rahwan, an expert in information systems and director at the Max Planck Institute for Human Development, told news magazine Der Spiegel.

Last year, locals in Berlin who were protesting against Google opening a campus in their neighbourhood gleefully drew parallels when the US company was rumoured to be considering moving into former Stasi headquarters.

And – opening an exhibition in Berlin in June 2019 – Roland Jahn, the federal commissioner for the Stasi Records Archive, confirmed that his office saw "the archive of Stasi files as a monument to the misuse of data".

This is part of the reason why Germany has been at the forefront of both national and European-wide attempts to regulate data-harvesting digital giants such as Facebook and Google.

In 2018, a study by consultancy Ernst and Young found that Germany had been the most active in Europe in imposing fines related to the European General Data Protection Regulation, fining 42 violators and issuing warnings to another 58.

CREDIT: Patrick George/Ikon

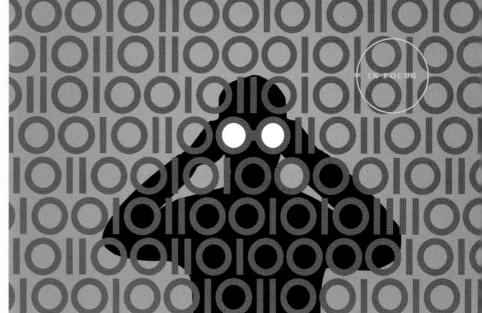

The plan by the German Federal Cartel Office to change the way Facebook does business by using national law on monopolies – have had worldwide resonance. The office forbade Facebook to combine German users' data from the three social platforms it owns – Facebook, Instagram and Whatsapp – because of worries about the resulting power. In effect, they were "breaking up" the company's data collection abilities. "Germans understand that information is power, so their sensitivity to surveillance and data protection is very much alive now," argued Dagmar Hovestädt, head of communications for the Stasi Records Archive.

"There is a great deal of knowledge to be gained by studying a fully developed state system of surveillance, like the one the Stasi built. Even though it was not very digital, it was very data-hungry, unrestricted in its reach and uncontrolled by a parliament, the judiciary or public discourse," she explained. "And it could use the data any way it wanted."

But, as Christian Katzenbach, a senior researcher at the Alexander von Humboldt Institute for Internet and Society, points out, contemporary German fears about protecting personal information started before that – in West Germany.

"The German discourse on data protection started in the 1960s in West Germany and culminated there in the early 1980s, around the national census of the time," he said.

In 1983, West Germans were supposed to answer detailed questions for a national census. But Germany's National Socialists, the Nazis, had used similar information to lethal effect when they were in power.

Germany's baby boomers, the '68ers, were coming to terms with the previous generation's collusion with the Nazi government and the 1983 attempt to collate this kind of information led to nationwide criticism and calls to boycott the process.

In the end, a legal challenge to the project

Some online platforms know more about us than the Stasi knew about their citizens

went all the way to Germany's highest court, which eventually ruled that aspects of the census violated a constitutional right to privacy and what Germans call "*informationelle Selbstbestimmung*". That's "informational self-determination" – something the court described as a fundamental right in a democratic society.

Today, those twin cultural currents – from East and West German experiences around privacy and personal information – are still having an impact on local attitudes. This is something the country's interior minister, whose plans for surveillance are currently still being negotiated with other ministries, may find hard to overcome. "The interior ministry came forward with a bill that was immature," said Thorsten Wetzling, of the Berlin-based think-tank Stiftung Neue Verantwortung. "And it was soundly rejected by other parties, including the justice ministry. They were told to come back with a new version. We don't know what the new bill will look like yet, but we can only assume that it may contain even stronger surveillance measures." ⊗

Cathrin Schaer is a freelance journalist based in Berlin, Germany

Freestyle portraits

Rachael Jolley introduces the work of three cartoonists from different countries who have been asked to illustrate freedom of expression themes

48(03): 54/55 I DOI: 10.1177/0306422019875094

CARTOONISTS ARE OFTEN in the firing line. They poke their pens at the outrageous behaviour of the powerful so responses can be angry – and in some cases life threatening. Cartoonists sometimes face prison for their work, and one who has been punished in this way is Musa Kart, in Turkey. Kart was informed he would be required to go to prison for one year and 16 days. He handed himself in and is now detained.

Pressure also comes from employers and publishers. Rob Rogers, a cartoonist for 25 years at the US city daily Pittsburgh Post-Gazette, lost his job last year. He told The Guardian that he believed this related to his searing portraits of US President Donald Trump. Pittsburgh mayor Bill Peduto, who had been the subject of Rogers's pen over the years, said the situation sent the "wrong message" about press freedom.

A Canadian newspaper came under fire recently for letting another cartoonist go over. Michael de Adder said all his cartoons relating to Trump over the past year had been rejected by the newspaper. The news company denied the matters were related.

For this issue, we asked three cartoonists, Pedro X Molina, Kanika Mishra and Badiucao, who are based in different parts of the world, to tackle the subject of threats to free expression from their own angles. ⊗

LEFT: Kanika Mishra is a cartoonist and animator who is known for creating India's first cartoon woman character, Karnika Kahen. She has faced rape and murder threats related to her work. She was the first woman to win a prestigious award for Courage in Cartooning from Cartoonists Rights Network, International

RIGHT: Chinese dissident artist Badiucao now lives in Australia where he confronts a variety of social and political issues head on in his cartoons and illustration work. He uses his art to challenge censorship and the control of the Communist Party in China, and for many years kept his identity secret. This year – on the 30th anniversary of the Tiananmen Square killings – he removed his mask to show who he was

RIGHT: Pedro X Molina is a Nicaraguan cartoonist and illustrator with a career spanning more than 20 years in the Nicaraguan and international media. His recent prizes include the Courage in Cartooning Award 2018 from Cartoonists Rights Network, International; Excellence in Journalism Award 2018 (cartoon category) from the Inter American Press Association; and The Maria Moors Cabot Award 2019, (the oldest international awards in the field of journalism) from Columbia University

www.pxmolina.com
pxmolina@guegue.com

Tackling news stories that journalists aren't writing

Alison Flood talks to bestselling crime writers **Val McDermid**, **Scott Turow**, **Massimo Carlotto** and **Ahmet Altan** about why they have used fiction to tell stories that would otherwise not have been heard

48(03): 56/59 I DOI: 10.1177/0306422019875096

BEFORE JOHN GRISHAM made his name with legal thrillers such as A Time to Kill and The Firm, he was working up to 70 hours a week in a small law practice in Mississippi.

Before Stieg Larsson posthumously achieved great fame as the author of The Girl with the Dragon Tattoo, he was reporting on anti-fascism in Sweden.

From John Mortimer, the barrister and free-speech defender who dreamed up Rumpole of the Bailey, to Robert Harris, who was a correspondent for the BBC and political editor of UK newspaper The Observer before writing thrillers including Fatherland and Enigma, the shelves in the crime sections in bookshops are packed with novels by authors with a social conscience who use fiction to open up stories which are not being told.

Bestselling crime novelist Val McDermid was a reporter for papers including the Daily Record in Glasgow and the Sunday People in Manchester. During this time she wrote about two of the UK's most notorious killing sprees – the Yorkshire Ripper and the Moors murders. She began writing crime while she was a journalist, learning a lot, she says, from the People's

investigative team –"How you dig, how you get beneath the surface, how you find ways to the truth that you don't necessarily have a need for in day-to-day news journalism," she told Index.

She also discovered "the frustration of spending a long time on an investigation that gets killed by the lawyers because they run scared of it". One report she worked on looked into a pregnancy-testing clinic that was giving a "disturbingly high" rate of false positives. The team discovered, says McDermid, that the women with the false positives were then being funnelled to a particular abortion clinic owned by the husband of the woman who owned the pregnancy testing clinic. It was a case of "join the dots" but, she says, the "legal team ran scared because essentially we were accusing doctors of complicity in this".

The story was not published in the newspaper but McDermid told Index: "I used the guts of that in one of the Kate Brannigan novels. Of course, they got brought down, the good guys won. That for me was one of the great joys of writing fiction – that I could tell some stories that had slipped between the cracks for one reason or another, and tell them in such a way that probably the people involved in it would have recognised it, but insufficient to get me sued for libel."

McDermid has a particularly notorious example of this. In her early days as a journalist she was sent to interview Jimmy Savile and found him to be a "deeply unpleasant man, but you couldn't say that, you had to go with the myth of Jimmy Savile".

Working in Manchester, there were also "several instances of people contacting us to claim they had been abused by Savile", but the difficulty was there was never any corroborative evidence, and often, she says, these were people who were damaged by what had happened to them and there was no way they could have been put in the witness box – it would have been an act of cruelty.

So she filed the stories away "in the back of my head".

But on a visit to America in the mid-1990s,

CREDIT: Alex Williamson/Ikon

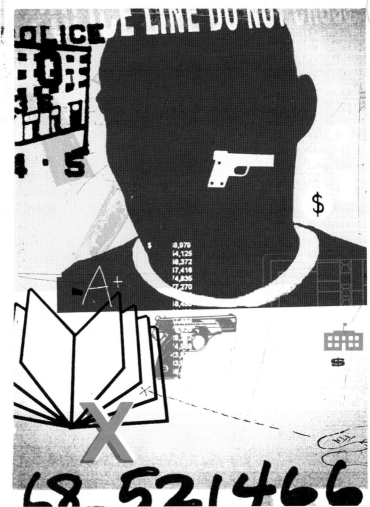

during the OJ Simpson trial, she met a woman whose company had been involved in the first allegations of paedophilia against Michael Jackson, and she came away thinking "celebrity was the new shield. That if you were famous enough you could get away with anything", and that she would write about this.

She created the character of Jacko Vance, a villain who appears in novels including The Wire in the Blood. "He's a former athlete who has a television programme called Vance's Visits. That was when Savile's Travels was still on the telly. He does charity work, visits hospital patients. Nobody made the connection," she said. "I knew how litigious Savile was and I really didn't want to lose all my money. It was only after Savile died that I felt able to respond when people asked – to say 'yes'."

There is a sense, McDermid says, that fiction can be used to tell stories that could not be told in the media at the time they were happening.

"However we do it, there are things for all sorts of reasons you can't tell in journalism or documentary form that the writer of fiction can plunder," she said.

American crime novelist Scott Turow is the author of 11 bestselling novels, but is best known for the multi-million seller Presumed Innocent, the story of Chicago prosecutor Rusty Sabich, who stands accused of raping and murdering a colleague with whom he has had an affair. Turow is also a lawyer, specialising in criminal litigation, and has continued to practise while writing.

His debut book was the memoir One L, about being at Harvard Law School.

"Going to law school was the great break of my literary career, not just because I ended up with a contract to write a book about my experience," he said. "But also because in going to law school I'd discovered a route to questions that were very much at my core, about differentiating right from wrong, and the difficulty of ever fully categorising human behaviour in ways that are just."

Turow's novels explore the fallibility of the legal system and how the black and white →

There are things for all sorts of reasons you can't tell in journalism or documentary form that the writer of fiction can plunder

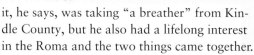

That for me was one of the great joys of writing fiction – that I could tell some stories that had slipped between the cracks

CREDIT: (top) Daniela Zedda (left) Geoff Pugh/Shutterstock (right) Alan Peebles (centre) ABC Ajansi/Shutterstock

→ results of a trial play out against the many shades of grey which is real life.

This, he says, has always been key for him. When he met Sydney Pollack to talk about the film of Presumed Innocent, Pollack told Turow he could name one thing he didn't want them to lose in the translation to film. "I said, 'the shades of grey'," Turow told Index. "Life is usually far more complex, and a poorer fit for the boxes the law of necessity has to make."

More recently, Turow has moved away from his fictional setting of Kindle County to replace domestic murders with war crimes in Testimony, taking on a wider canvas and looking more closely at a different kind of atrocity.

ABOVE: Italian crime author and playwright Massimo Carlotto

BELOW: American author and lawyer Scott Turow in Lincoln's Inn Fields, London where traditionally barristers have their chambers

This time, his prosecutor is confronted with an alleged massacre of 400 Roma in Bosnia in 2004. Part of it, he says, was taking "a breather" from Kindle County, but he also had a lifelong interest in the Roma and the two things came together.

"I came to greatly respect the mission of the International Criminal Court, which has exposed some deficiencies in US foreign policy, even before the current administration," Turow told Index. "I loved the learning that went into the book."

Turow agrees that fiction can be a way of looking at difficult themes in more detail, and appealing to a different audience, than a straight piece of non-fiction might.

"I think fiction works from ambiguity, what Faulkner called 'the human heart in conflict with itself'," he said. "The genius of fiction, over and above film, or even journalism, is that it dwells so deeply within the character. Fiction works from the inside out, and film the reverse. Journalism is also supposed to be objective, so it's much more about the outer view of people."

Massimo Carlotto was a reporter before he witnessed a brutal murder – a murder he didn't commit but which led to years spent in Italian prison before an international campaign saw him pardoned. Once he was freed, Carlotto turned to crime fiction, dreaming up his investigator "the Alligator". The series is published in English by Europa Editions, and is becoming a major proponent of "Mediterranean noir".

Fiction, Carlotto told Index, is "democratic, open to all, and allows the writer to tell things the Italian press won't publish".

"I decided to write fiction because it's a genre I love very much," he said. "In my novels I delve deep into the links between organised crime and financial, political and monetary power: Italy's system. The readers are completely aware of this."

He is not sure if he would have taken the

step into novel-writing if he hadn't been imprisoned for seven years, but admits that "having been a guest of the Italian state has allowed me to get to know many criminals, and as a result I've been to tell their stories more realistically than other writers may have done".

Carlotto draws from real life – real criminals, real killings – to tell his stories. He does this, he says, because the relationship between crime and society has changed.

"Nowadays, mafias and organised crime are no longer confined to the margins but have infiltrated much of society. In a break with the past, they want to have real influence," he said. "This is why they invest in politics. Just this week two politicians from two different regions of Italy were arrested and accused of being linked to the 'Ndrangheta, the Calabrese mafia. Today, organised crime is involved in illegal waste disposal and food adulteration, in effect jeopardising people's health. These are all very good reasons to tell readers, by means of compelling plots and good writing, of the sad reality in which we live."

Globalisation "has caused a historic, momentous revolution in organised crime". This makes it particularly important to him to expose criminal activity in his fiction. "We find a number of criminal activities behind every global phenomenon: migration, pollution, finance... so goes the world," he said.

Turkish author and journalist Ahmet Altan explores, in his literary noir novel Endgame, the ways in which corruption envelops Turkish life. He describes it as a novel which "brings a journalist's observations into the world of a novelist".

"If you look at the great classics closely, you'll see that most of them are developed versions of newspaper stories," he said. "The literary worth of a novel depends on the skill of the novelist, but its story is nothing but a news story. A journalist informs you about what happened; a novelist tells you the story of the emotional world behind what happened."

Altan's historical novels are also highly political – his Ottoman Quartet spans the half-century before the rise of Mustafa Kemal Atatürk, the founder of the Turkish Republic. "When you look back at people's greed, their hunger for power, their desire to rule... the absurdity of all of these becomes even more evident," he told Index, from prison. An exclusive English language extract of Altan's novel The Longest Night was recently published in the magazine (Index vol 48.2, p84). Altan was sentenced to life in prison in 2016. In early July, his life sentence was overturned, with the case due to be reheard by a lower court. He said that while in prison he had written a new novel, called Lady Life. "My life in prison hasn't shaped or influenced this novel. I have exhausted my literary ties to prison by writing my latest book of essays, I Will Never See the World Again," he said. "I don't think I'll go back to the subject." ⊛

ABOVE: Scottish crime-writer Val McDermid

CENTRE: Turkish novelist and journalist Ahmet Altan who is in jail for criticising the government

Alison Flood is a freelance writer who specialises in writing about books and authors

In going to law school I'd discovered a route to questions that were very much at my core, about differentiating right from wrong

Mosul's new chapter

Isis burnt thousands of books in Mosul's central library, writes **Omar Mohammed**, founder of the news blog Mosul Eye, who talks to students about the importance of rebuilding it

48(03): 60/61 I DOI: 10.1177/0306422019875093

IT'S A SMALL green building with two black doors which does not warrant a second look.

But that unremarkable building is the temporary location of the destroyed central library of the University of Mosul. Inside are thousands of books which have been donated from around the world.

The original library and its contents were destroyed by Isis after they captured Mosul in 2014. It was a bid to wipe out the city's history and intellectual heritage.

Now the library is being rebuilt and starting to provide services to the university's students and researchers. Ahmad al-Najim, a student of economic studies, believes the library is essential – not just to students but to the recovery of his city as a whole.

"The library is the face of Mosul. We need the library to protect and preserve our history to envision our future," he said.

Another student Yusif Ali adds that the library is "the only place where we can make a better future". For many students on campus, the library is vital for research and to develop their knowledge.

Last May, I was invited by a Danish anthropologist to an event in Norway – the fifth anniversary of the Future Library, a self-defined "100-year public artwork" tasked with collecting an original literary text by a renowned writer every year from 2014 to 2114, which will remain unread and unpublished until 2114.

The idea that a library would open in

a century's time was fascinating to me, someone who was trying to revive his own library destroyed by a group of terrorists. The Future Library confirmed our mission to rebuild the library of Mosul, as there are still those who imagine and believe in the power of libraries.

At that event, in the Nordmarka Forest, just outside Oslo, I sat listening to South Korean writer Han Kang reading aloud. While the audience was focused on her words, my mind was half a world away in Mosul, consumed by thoughts of whether our once thriving library would ever recover.

Since the first days of its occupation of Mosul, Isis wanted to change the city's history and replace it with its own narrative. The first victim of that destructive ideology was our library. They stole rare manuscripts, burned irreplaceable books and destroyed a building which once had one of the most extensive collections of documents and archives in the entire Middle East.

In the battle for the city, more than 80% of the urban landscape was heavily damaged or completely destroyed. Although the need to reconstruct the city was pressing, the library was also an urgent priority for many Mosul residents, including Ali al-Baroodi, an English teacher at Mosul University.

"We need libraries, as most of them were either burned, bombed or looted. It breaks my heart to walk by empty bookshelves and blackened walls," he said. "We also need to revive school library visits so that we'll have a new generation that loves and values reading."

These convictions were the force behind the launch of a global campaign in February 2017 to

preserve the library's remaining books, as well as to resupply it.

The idea behind this campaign goes well beyond the books themselves. It is also about engaging the city's youth who, for three years, lived under the rule of constant terror and experienced indescribable horrors. I called upon young people in Mosul to help us recover the library's remaining books, and the results were amazing. We preserved more than 30,000 rare books and manuscripts.

The global response was also immense as thousands of people responded to the call, sending us books. In less than a month, Mosul Eye's appeal reached its first goal – that of reconnecting Mosul with the world.

The campaign re-inspired Mosul's cosmopolitan character and its intellectual and cultural life, showing the world that a city once occupied by Isis that should be starving was also yearning for books. But there were those who attacked, mocked and humiliated me and others who were calling for books for a destroyed city, and who told us we first needed bread.

We wanted to do much more than restock our library with books, however.

I visited libraries around the world, including the Alliance Israelite Universelle Library in Paris – a library dedicated to preserving Jewish history – in an effort to obtain digital copies of rare manuscripts, documents and microfilms. I

CREDIT: Zaid Al-Obeidi/AFP/Getty

The library is the face of Mosul. We need the library to protect and preserve our history to envision our future

also spent countless hours searching open access collections in an effort to collect any document related to Mosul and its history and my work as a historian helped me gain access to many other libraries and institutions.

The linking of diverse partners round the world including in the Middle East and north Africa was made easier by new technology and brought us different books from many places. The campaign for libraries is about people and creating a new collective and visual memory in Mosul, especially among the youth, and ending the censorship of reading in the city.

"We cannot have a university or a city without a library," agriculture professor Anas al-Taie said.

More books arrive at Mosul every day, but our focus is now moving to digitisation, so that what has survived these years of war and destruction will be protected. We are reconnecting the university and its library with the growing field of digital humanities to provide access to the most recent publications and digitised materials.

Our call is now for donations of digital archives, digitised manuscripts and assistance with establishing a digitisation unit.

After so many years of isolation and disconnection from the rest of the world, Mosul is being reconnected globally through books.

These budding relationships and the future projects they will yet build are starting, slowly, to replace the terrible memories of these past years, especially for the young generation. ⊗

*Additional research by **Angela Boskovitch***

***Omar Mohammed** is a historian and the founder of Mosul Eye*

LEFT: Raghad Hammadi, a member of a group of students who campaigned for the Central Library of Mosul University to be rebuilt, walks in the rubble and destruction in May 2018. Isis fighters looted and systematically destroyed book collections in the library during February 2015

The [REDACTED] crossword

Clues by **Herbashe**. Answers p34

48(03): 62/62 I DOI: 10.1177/0306422019875097

SEVEN OF THE answers are names related by a theme that's central to this magazine. Aptly enough, their definitions have been expunged, leaving only wordplay to figure out those seven clues. In addition the shaded letters (plus another answer from the grid, repeated twice) can be rearranged to form a relevant quote from one of the seven names

Quote word lengths: 10,3,3,2,(2 down),9,4,(2 down).

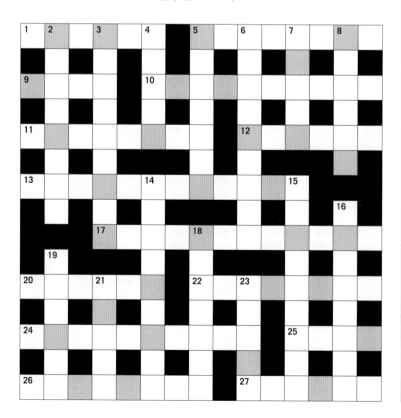

ACROSS

1 Cultural value system that embraces 'normal' (6)
5 Spoken comment (8)
9 Ever-festering cut? (4)
10 Record collector has muscles and large vehicle (10)
11 Scottish island touched by greed, regularly plundered and settled (8)
12 Arch at centre of stage (6)
13 Harpist comes avant-garde, producing mood music (12)
17 Final letter admitted to sin, honestly recollecting (12)
20 Monday's beginning relatively poorly (6)
22 Stupid to get cornered by bull, perhaps (8)
24 Smart to restrain excited animal's rampaging (10)
25 Bland and meagre yam portion (4)
26 Fantastic rare find, it's found over a rainbow (8)
27 Show up directly from masquerade (6)

DOWN

2 Incomplete letter in Greek by biblical lady - it's sought by philosophers (3,5)
3 Commentators rant and roar about society, primarily (9)
4 Display picture, getting copyright first (5)
5 Make haste to depart (7)
6 American remains taken care of under this occupation? (9)
7 Flamboyantly wears diamonds (5)
8 Card game joined, not for purposes of paying debt. (6)
14 Animal in novel or parable (5,4)
15 No longer prone to enlarge after mealtime (7,2)
16 Mountains and burning hill noticed when looking upwards (8)
18 Bound to keep to one's own level (3-4)
19 Huge weight advanced by very short distance (6)
21 Deep in French, more dull in English (5)
23 Trickster's accent with no origin (5)

Cries from the last century and lessons for today

Sally Gimson introduces **Emilie Pine**, **Elif Shafak**, **Kerry Hudson** and **Nicholas Hytner** who give their takes on plays and writings from some of Index's greatest past contributors

48(03): 63/67 I DOI: 10.1177/0306422019875099

MANY OF THE great Western writers and artists of the 20th century were marked by dictatorship, authoritarianism and censorship. And Index on Censorship magazine has published their work since its launch in 1972.

For this issue, we have taken plays by Samuel Beckett and Václav Havel, an address by Nadine Gordimer and an essay by Arthur Miller, all published in this magazine in the 1970s and 1980s, and asked contemporary writers Emilie Pine, Elif Shafak, Kerry Hudson and theatre director Nicholas Hytner to give us their reactions.

All four of the past authors were personally affected by government actions which directly threatened them and sought to curtail their freedom of expression: Beckett in Nazi-occupied France, Gordimer in apartheid South Africa, Havel in communist Czechoslovakia and Miller in the anti-communist McCarthy trials of 1950s USA.

Shafak is the only one of our contemporary writers who has direct experience of living in a country, Turkey, where writers, artists and academics are imprisoned. But all four have insights about how the impact of free speech being closed down. Pine revels in Beckett's brilliance at portraying small gestures of resistance. While both Hudson and Hytner look at how Havel and Miller understood how the powerful distort reality to hide the truth. ⊗

***Sally Gimson** is deputy editor of Index on Censorship magazine.*

Additional research by ***Sophia Paley***

CREDIT: Robin Heighway-Bury/Ikon

BRINGING IDEAS OUT OF QUARANTINE

Turkish novelist ELIF SHAFAK sees parallels between the isolation from intellectual ideas NADINE GORDIMER describes in apartheid South Africa and the information bubbles of today's digital world

WORDS ARE HEAVY in my motherland, Turkey. I come from a country where every author, poet, academic and journalist knows that because of an article, an interview, a poem, a novel or even a retweet, you may find yourself in trouble with the authorities.

Your books can be seized by police officers and investigated by prosecutors while sentences are plucked from your texts, circulated all over social media by thousands of bots and trolls and eventually used as "evidence" in a courtroom. You may easily get arrested, sentenced or exiled. Imagination is regarded as an act of outspoken defiance in undemocratic regimes. Writing about taboos is the hardest – whether they be political, cultural or sexual.

In a climate of growing fear and intimidation, there is not only top-down censorship but also a widespread self-censorship. How does censorship work as part of the grand design of systematic discrimination, human rights violations and oppression? This is the question that the brilliant writer and political activist Nadine Gordimer tackles in her address, and she does so with wisdom, courage and integrity. Although she addresses a particular moment in time and a specific location (South Africa from 1948 to the early 1990s), her words are strikingly relevant for all of us anywhere in the world today. In the age of growing populist nationalism and its next-in line, populist authoritarianism, there will be more and more writers and poets who, one way or another, find themselves dealing with censorship (or self-censorship), just like there will be more and more of us catapulted into a state of exile (or self-imposed exile).

Much has been said about what happens to the state apparatus or the structure of politics and the character of politicians under oppressive regimes. What is a bit harder to talk about is what happens to society when freedoms are lost, diversity is crushed and segregation and discrimination are institutionalised.

Yet this was the question that preoccupied many east European intellectuals such as the Polish writer and poet Czesław Miłosz. It is a question that preoccupies Gordimer as she shows how the apartheid regime permeates every aspect of daily life.

Imagine generation after generation growing up in a climate in which critical-minded artists and writers, from the Martinique French political philosopher Frantz Fanon to the Kenyan-born American academic Ali Mazrui, are either banned or silenced and a large number of books by African authors are expurgated. The thing about censorship is that it's not only pervasive but also *insatiate* – unable to stop. It aims not only at books that deal with political issues but also at books that explore the complexity of the human condition, stories that promote empathy and understanding of others.

In times of apathy and lands of autocracy, empathy is often regarded as an act of defiance.

The intellectual isolation and epistemic quarantine that Gordimer observed in apartheid South Africa is not a thing of the past. In the age of digital tribes and political clans we are being pushed into "either-or" dualities and clashing certainties. Different people get their sources of information from different channels and therefore believe in alternate "realities", while truth is being attacked and eroded systematically. We live in a world in which there is too much information, very little knowledge and even less wisdom.

Censorship, abundant information (and disinformation) and continuous apathy... they all numb us inside, little by little, day by day. We become desensitised. After a while, we do not really register the news, we just scroll up and down. After a while, numbers do not mean a thing – whether it's 5,000 refugees or 500,000 refugees, we stop feeling the pain of others; we stop caring. And that is the most dangerous threshold.

If enough people have become sufficiently numb, upon that fertile ground authoritarian narratives can sow the seeds of all kinds of racism, sexism, xenophobia and discrimination.

Censorship succeeds not when books are banned or authors are put in prison but when readers stop reading. When people become uninterested, disconnected, desensitised. The long fight for a pluralistic, democratic and truly egalitarian future must therefore always rely on inclusion, empathy, diversity and connectivity.

Elif Shafak is a Turkish novelist and her novel 10 Minutes 38 Seconds in this Strange World has been longlisted for the Booker prize

ABOVE: Writer Elif Shafak

APARTHEID AND 'THE PRIMARY HOMELAND'

Nadine Gordimer

This is the text of an address given earlier this year in South Africa which illustrates some of the problems connected with the South African government's plans to abolish the right of appeal against decisions brought by the State Publications Control Board.

Since 1969 the South African Government, egged on by the General Synod of the Nederduits Gereformeerde Kerk, has threatened to abolish the right of appeal to the Supreme Court against decisions of the publications Control Board — the government-appointed censors. With the appointment of a new, political hardliner as Minister of the Interior last August, there is perhaps less chance than ever that the threat will not become a reality. An interdepartmental government

APARTHEID AND "THE PRIMARY HOMELAND"
By Nadine Gordimer, September 1972, vol. 1, issue: 3-4
Nadine Gordimer (1923-2014) was a Nobel Prize-winning South African novelist and activist who, for much of her life, was engaged in the literary struggle against apartheid. Index published her articles until a few years before her death. Under apartheid, Gordimer's novels Burger's Daughter and July's People were banned.

CREDIT: Zeynel Abidin

WHAT IT IS TO BE UNSEEN

Academic and writer EMILIE PINE reflects on SAMUEL BECKETT's play Catastrophe and the power of the silenced to face down their oppressors

SAMUEL BECKETT'S **C**ATASTROPHE, first performed in 1982 at the Avignon Theatre Festival, in France, and first published in 1984 in Index on Censorship magazine, has long stood as a testament to the power of small gestures of resistance.

Written in support of the writer Václav Havel, then imprisoned in Czechoslovakia, Catastrophe exposes how routinely the rights of the disenfranchised can be abused, while also allowing us to hope – revealing the subversive and startling authority of the victim who dares to look back at his oppressors.

The play consists of a lone performer (P) standing on a block, with a director (D) who orchestrates P's movements, aided by his female assistant (A). The director's treatment of both his assistant and the performer – "Step on it, I have a caucus", "Down his head" – projects his total authority over them. Though set in a theatre, there are suggestions throughout the play of Beckett's deliberate evocation of the still all-too-familiar tropes of tyrannical regimes.

D's direction to "whiten" P's skin implies the erasure of individual – and racial – identity; P's pyjama costume hints that he has been taken from his home during the night, his clenched hands imply coercion; the spotlight trained upon P is reminiscent of interrogation techniques; and A's collaboration with D illustrates the failure of solidarity between subjected groups. Most of all, D's angry instruction that P utter "not a squeak" illustrates the enforced silencing of the subjugated "other". Though we may have forums today that act as loudspeakers for silenced voices, this instruction still resonates chillingly for me, knowing that there are so many people for whom free speech is still an impossibility.

Throughout D and A's deliberations about creating a spectacle of catastrophe, P stands with head abjectly bowed, enduring their manipulations and derogations. And at the end, as recorded applause begins, it seems as if P has indeed been obliterated in the quest for catastrophe.

Yet the protagonist does not submit. Instead, at the end of the play he "raises his head" and "fixes the audience" with his gaze. In response, the applause "falters" then "dies". P is victorious in his disruption of both the spectacle of his suffering and the director's power.

Perhaps most revolutionary for me, and still relevant today, is the power of the attention that P commands at the end. In Beckett's first play, Waiting for Godot, the character Vladimir appeals to a witness: "Tell him ... [He hesitates] ... tell him you saw us. [Pause.] You did see us, didn't you?"

This painful demand resonates throughout all of Beckett's theatre work as he stages the human need to be seen and validated by an external witness.

This is what P requires at the end of Catastrophe. The attention of the audience not only recognises the necessity of resistance to tyranny, but the equal necessity of witnessing acts of resistance. Beckett's play gave Havel, cloistered and invisible in prison, the strength to endure because it revealed to him that he was not unseen. In witnessing Havel and the unnamed "P", Catastrophe illustrates the vital role of engaged and active audiences who applaud not the catastrophe but the act of resistance.

This play is not a historical document. Although the world today is different to the one that Beckett used as his backdrop, the global stage is still marked by oppressive regimes that silence those who dare to have a different point of view.

The solidarity that is unavailable to P during the play may, however, be granted these days through the work of magazines such as Index, organisations such as Amnesty, and the simple power of embodied and digital connections that we have seen change systems. It is only through this kind of work, through speaking out and listening when others speak out in turn, that we can create spaces in which both the individual and the collective can be witnessed, and can act as witnesses.

Emilie Pine is an associate professor of modern drama at University College, Dublin, Ireland and author of the essay collection Notes to Self

---

Samuel Beckett
Catastrophe
For Václav Havel

In a letter to Samuel Beckett written in April 1983, six weeks after his release, the Czech dramatist Václav Havel described 'the shock I experienced during my time in prison when, on the occasion of one of her one-hour visits allowed four times a year, my wife told me in the presence of an obtuse warder that at Avignon there took place a night of solidarity with me, and that you took the opportunity to write, and to make public for the first time, your play Catastrophe. For a long time afterwards there accompanied me in prison a great joy

---

LEFT: Author Emilie Pine

CATASTROPHE: FOR VÁCLAV HAVEL
By Samuel Beckett, February 1984, vol. 13, issue: 1

Samuel Beckett (1906-89) won the Nobel Prize in Literature in 1969. The Irish playwright and critic is best known for his plays Waiting for Godot, Endgame and Krapp's Last Tape as well as his novel Molloy. He wrote in both French and English and spent much of his life in France.

CREDIT: Ruth Campbell

WE ARE STILL TEMPTED

Novelist KERRY HUDSON considers VÁCLAV HAVEL's play Temptation and what it says to us today

CZECH PLAYWRIGHT VÁCLAV Havel's play Temptation, a modern reworking of the Faust legend, shows us the impossibility of navigating an Escher-like totalitarian regime with anything resembling free will.

Havel, the non-conformist writer who would go on to become the first president of Czechoslovakia in 1989, conceived of Temptation, first published in Index on Censorship magazine, while he was in prison. It was here he later recounted he felt "tempted by the authorities. I thought the devil was in me. I felt I had made a bad step [...] This trauma, this feeling that the devil was around me, stayed with me".

Years after leaving prison, he was seized to write the play within 10 days, after which he descended into two days of extreme sickness.

In 2019, the play resonates as it must have when it debuted in 1986. Certainly, it helps that Havel modelled his own Faust, Foustka, on his personal experience so that even as he duplicitously tries to squirm himself out of one corner into another, he is empathetic, flawed and deeply relatable.

Havel had stated that his was a play about choices. Foustka's choice is whether to carefully dance (often literally at work socials) around the banal, narrow-minded, double-think of the Institute of Science at which he works, or to go over entirely to the black magic offered by the Mephistopheles-like character, Fistula.

Perhaps the most interesting aspect of reading this play on the page is how Havel crafts his language to replicate the structural confines that each "choice" represents to Foustka. Where the institute scenes feature long, pointless speeches, multiple repetitions, frequent jostling for position and status, the scenes where Foustka converses with Fistula are concise, witty and often cuttingly cruel.

As a woman reading this play decades later it would be remiss of me not to say that the depiction of women within this regime is very much through Havel's unrelenting male gaze. A female scientist who, though wearing a white coat, spends most of the scenes at the Institute looking into a compact. A young secretary who is used as a sexual foil is then cast out. Even Vilma, Foustka's partner, spends much of her time running around in a lace negligee begging to be subjugated and beaten for sexual pleasure. Perhaps the intention was to show that women will always end up the worst off and even a totalitarian regime is still, essentially, a man's world, but this aspect aged far less well than the rest of the narrative which feels, sadly, timelier than ever.

Of course, there is no real choice for Foustka and it emerges that, in fact, the Director of the Institute has been working with his "friend of long standing", Fistula, all along. The machinations of power were always bigger than Foustka, no matter what freedoms he naively assumed.

As Boris Johnson becomes the leader of the Conservative Party and UK prime minister without a general election and US President Donald Trump nods happily along to baying cries of "send them home" at rallies, one can't help thinking that we must have invoked the devil ourselves, and with the help of Haajah, "the spirit of politics", that we too have been robbed, or given up, all of our assumed choices just like Foustka.

Kerry Hudson is the author of Lowborn. Her second novel Thirst won the Prix Femina Étranger

Years after leaving prison, he was seized to write the play within 10 days, after which he descended into two days of extreme sickness

ABOVE: Author Kerry Hudson

INDEX ON CENSORSHIP 10/86

Václav Havel TEMPTATION

Václav Havel

TEMPTATION

A play in ten scenes

For Zdeněk Urbánek

Dr Henry FOUSTKA, *scientist*
FISTULA, *invalid in retirement*
The DIRECTOR
VILMA, *scientist*
The DEPUTY DIRECTOR
MAGGIE, *secretary*
Dr Libuše LORENCOVÁ, *scientist*
Dr Vilém KOTRLÝ, *scientist*
Dr Alois NEUWIRTH, *scientist*
Mrs HOUBOVÁ, *Foustka's landlady*
DANCER *(male)*
PETRUŠKA
SECRETARY
FIRST LOVER
SECOND LOVER

SCENE ONE   *(The Institute)*
SCENE TWO   *(Foustka's flat)*

TEMPTATION: A PLAY IN 10 SCENES

By Václav Havel, November 1986, vol. 15, issue: 10

The Czechoslovakian playwright and poet Václav Havel (1936-2011) was also a political dissident under communism, and spent four years in prison for his work. He was often published in Index magazine. In 1989 he led the Velvet Revolution and became president of Czechoslovakia in December that year

CREDIT: Nick Turner

THERE IS WORSE TO COME

NICHOLAS HYTNER believes ARTHUR MILLER was more optimistic about the powerful than Shakespeare, who better understood the ways of today's populist leaders

ARTHUR MILLER HOPED in his essay for Index that, despite everything, "a healthy scepticism towards the powerful has at last become second nature to the great mass of people almost everywhere".

We have regressed.

In William Shakespeare's Julius Caesar, the "great mass" of the Roman people are suckers for the powerful.

"The sin of power," writes Miller, is "to convince people that the false is true".

Caesar refuses the crown three times. The Republican elite knows what he's up to. One of them dismisses the mob's applause with contempt: "If Caesar had stabbed their mothers they would have done no less."

To be fair, Caesar doesn't make this claim on his own behalf, unlike US President Donald Trump who boasted during the 2016 election campaign that he could shoot somebody in the middle of Fifth Avenue without losing any voters.

The attachment of the Roman senators to their institutions is fiercer than our own. To protect their ancient privileges they murder Caesar, persuading the incorruptible Brutus to lead them. Some of them want to murder Caesar's cheerleader, Mark Antony, too, but Brutus – who wants the conspirators to appear "to the common eyes" as purgers, not murderers – won't have it. Convinced of his own rectitude, he goes on to allow Mark Antony to speak after him at Caesar's funeral. It does not occur to him that "reality is quite simply the arena into which determined men can enter and reshape just about every kind of relationship in it".

Brutus's funeral oration, which celebrates Caesar as it justifies his assassination, is rational and rhetorically impressive. But when he cedes the stage to Mark Antony, a fabulous storyteller, he is routed.

"I am no orator," says Antony, "but, as you know me all, a plain, blunt man." It's the least of his fabrications. He describes Caesar's murder in thrilling, gory detail, though he doesn't let on that he wasn't there to witness it. He produces Caesar's will and promises every Roman a handout of 75 drachmas. Whatever it takes. UK prime minister Boris Johnson promised £350 million a week for the National Health Service as a Brexit dividend. He's an enthusiastic student of Shakespeare, so he'll know that the 75 drachmas never materialises. Job done, Antony has Caesar's will altered: he needs the money to wage civil war.

The heirs of Mark Antony (heirs at least of his dishonesty, demagoguery, narcissism and sexual incontinence) are in charge now. It is they who, in Miller's words, "distort and falsify the structures of reality".

Shakespeare offers no quick fix. One of the Roman plebeians predicts that after Caesar's violent death "there will a worse come in his place", which is spot on: the collapse of the Republic ushers in centuries of imperial despotism. Scepticism towards the powerful turns out to be less widespread than Miller hoped. Power has found a way of disguising itself, particularly online. Maybe somebody will work out how to respond with stories as good and as gripping as Antony's - stories that seek not to reshape reality but to explain it, stories that acknowledge the myriad conflicting claims on the world as it is.

Nicholas Hytner is a theatre director and producer and one of the founders of The Bridge theatre

> *The heirs of Mark Antony (heirs at least of his dishonesty, demagoguery, narcissism and sexual incontinence) are in charge now*

CREDIT: Dave J Hogan/Getty

Arthur Miller
The sin of power

It is always necessary to ask how old a writer is who is reporting his impressions of a social phenomenon. Like the varying depth of a lens, the mind bends the light passing through it quite differently according to its age. When I first experienced Prague in the late sixties, the Russians had only just entered with their armies; writers (almost all of them self-proclaimed Marxists if not Party members) were still unsure of their fate under the new occupation, and when some thirty or forty of them gathered in the office of *Listy* to 'interview' me, I could smell the apprehension among them. And indeed, many would soon be fleeing abroad, some would be jailed, and others would never again be permitted to publish in their native language. Incredibly, that was almost a decade ago.

But since the first major blow to the equanimity of my mind was the victory of Nazism, first in

ABOVE: Theatre director Nicholas Hytner

THE SIN OF POWER
By Arthur Miller, May 1978, vol. 7, issue: 3
American playwright Arthur Miller (1915-2005) wrote All My Sons, the Pulitzer Prize-winning Death of a Salesman, and The Crucible. Many of his plays were turned into Hollywood films. In 1956 Miller was called before the USA's House Committee on Un-American Activities but refused to name any alleged communist writers. He was convicted of contempt but appealed and won.

In memory of Andrew Graham-Yooll, 1944-2019

Index editor **Rachael Jolley** remembers former editor **Andrew Graham-Yooll**, who risked his life to report from Argentina during the worst years of the dictatorship

48(03): 68/69 | DOI: 10.1177/0306422019875095

ANDREW GRAHAM-YOOLL WOULD get in touch once a year as he planned his annual summer trip to the UK to visit his family. After leaving the role of editor in 1993, Andrew remained an enthusiast of Index on Censorship magazine and would always offer to drop in to the office to say "hello".

In the past six years I have seen him on a regular basis, but when he dropped in it wasn't to reminisce, Andrew was very much the working journalist right until the end. He always had an idea for a new story or a feature brewing, or was ready to update us on the latest news from Argentina. He didn't talk about the past unless we pushed him to do so. My regret now is that we didn't do that more often.

He told us his years at Index were "one of the most important steps in my life". He took the job as editor in 1989, after years of reporting from Argentina during a time when people who criticised the government were disappeared, murdered or jailed, and after fleeing the country with his family for his own safety.

One of the highlights of his years in the editor's chair was becoming the first publisher of Ariel Dorfman's play Death and the Maiden, which went on to become a worldwide success.

This summer I was looking forward to meeting up with Andrew again. Sadly it was not to be. On 6 July, we heard the news that he had died.

He never retired from journalism and had been bashing out columns for the Buenos Aires Times until just a few weeks earlier. The zest and determination to write something that might make a difference never left him.

During my time as editor, Andrew continued to write for Index about his beloved Argentina, and to criticise the things he thought needed to improve. We battled against the vagaries of the Argentinian postal system to get him copies of the magazine. Sometimes they arrived, sometimes they didn't.

In 2015 he wrote a piece that looked back at Argentina in the 1970s and 1980s as a context for a critique of 2015's politics. It started: "What does not change over the decades is the desire of those in power to limit information which might be unsuitable to their needs. Why should Argentina be different?"

That question is at the heart of everything that Index does, and resonates with those who battle for freedom of expression everywhere. Andrew nailed it in that first sentence.

He went on: "Nearly four decades ago, the military regime (1976-83) of General Jorge Rafael Videla went from threatening and terrorising journalists as a means of controlling

These were the 'disappeared' – the only record at the time, meticulously recorded by Andrew, and the reason for the junta's attempt on his life shortly before his departure

CREDITS: Cedoc/Perfil Archive/Graham-Yooll family

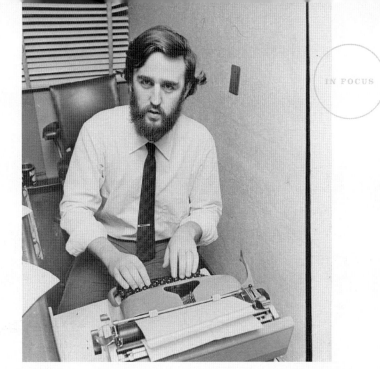

information to murdering them. More than 100 journalists were killed during the seven-year rule of the armed forces, but that figure was hardly reported in the establishment press."

His analysis of the power that Argentinian President Cristina Fernández de Kirchner held in 2015, and the techniques she used, should be mandatory reading for those who now worry about presidents Donald Trump, Vladimir Putin and Rodrigo Duterte. She was ahead of the game, and Andrew was watching.

He described how "aides of President Cristina Fernández de Kirchner have used contrived show trials, held on a stage in front of Government House, to 'try' well-known media personalities accused of siding with the military during the dictatorship".

And he argued that while Argentinian media were much freer to criticise than they had been in decades, "the government encouraged business allies and supporters to buy into existing companies, facilitating the purchases with generous credits and assuring proprietors abundant and well-paid government advertising".

Andrew continued to use his journalistic skills to expose scandals and excesses and was as committed to journalism as he was when he wrote for Index's second issue in 1973.

Through the years, Andrew reported on shootings and killings, infringements of press freedoms and the "disappeared". He kept detailed logs of incidents during the seven years of dictatorship and smuggled information to London. Another former editor, Judith Vidal-Hall, recalled: "In 1976, Andrew gave me a bulky package, asking that I take care of it in his absence. It was 1983-84 and he did well to be cautious – he was badly beaten up as he prepared to testify to the 'disappearances' under the military.

"On his return he opened the parcel – which I'd kept under my bed untouched – and showed me the documents inside. Long lists of names, dates, details he'd recorded between 1973 and his departure three years later. These were the 'disappeared' – the only record at the time, meticulously recorded by Andrew, and the

reason for the junta's attempt on his life shortly before his departure."

Andrew rarely talked about the risks he had to take, or about the danger. He preferred to talk about what was happening now, but his work is a reminder of what can happen, and why the media must report freely.

He would have loved the memorial party held at the Argentinian embassy in London in his honour on 22 July. A live tango band played, Malbec was swigged, and children ran from room to room. And there were speeches about the immense contribution that Andrew had made.

He would also have liked the words that Ariel Dorfman sent us honouring their friendship. "He was not only my friend but my editor," he said. "He published Death and the Maiden in Index, the first time it was ever printed. And that initiated my collaboration with Index, which I so value to this day. For a man on such a serious mission, of such vast courage, always so close to horror and death and sorrow, Andrew was vitality itself, with a wonderful smile and sense of humour. 'The bastards won't take joy away from us,' he once said to me. And now I'll repeat that and say that Death can't take the joy away from having been his *compañero*." ⊗

ABOVE AND LEFT:
Andrew Graham-Yooll as a young reporter

Rachael Jolley is the editor-in-chief of Index on Censorship

PICTURED: Speed control officers measuring how fast a lorry is driving in France

CREDIT: Philippe Le Tellier/Paris Match via Getty

CULTURE

Backed into a corner by love

Karoline Kan interviews censored Chinese author **Chen Xiwo** about the importance of family in China – even when it leads to abuse. Plus a new translation of his story Vita

48(03): 72/78 I DOI: 10.1177/0306422019874282

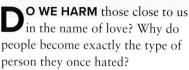

LEFT: Author Chen Xiwo

DO WE HARM those close to us in the name of love? Why do people become exactly the type of person they once hated?

In Vita, a short story from a collection of stories, Life and Fate, an extract of which is translated for the first time below, Chinese author Chen Xiwo tells of a twisted relationship between a mother and her daughter, and the blurred boundary between love and hatred. The woman in the story had a hard time giving birth to her daughter, Vita, who is blamed for all the misfortunes in her life: her poor health, her unhappy marriage and her economic difficulties.

At the same time, Vita is all the hope in her life. She provides her daughter with the best life and education she can afford, but also controls everything in her life. Vita loves and hates her mother, but ends up repeating her fate and failure. She even develops her mother's controlling personality and is abusive when the tables are turned and her mother needs her care.

"It is common to see Chinese people harm each other inside a family in the name of love," Chen told Index. "In many of the family arguments, the conclusion always goes like 'I am your parent, I gave birth to you, so you have to do this or that'. We don't have a sense of boundary in a close relationship."

Chen believes this phenomenon is related to Chinese culture, where most people believe that family is above anything and you should make sacrifices for their sake. In return, you have the right to expect your family to do anything for you.

Born in 1963, Chen is one of China's most controversial writers. He touches on social corruption, explores the elusive mental process and spiritual world, and reveals the complexity of human nature through sexual relationships. His novella I Love My Mum is about incest between a disabled mother and her son. It features in The Book of Sins, which was published in English in 2014 but is banned in China.

Chen has been battling with censorship since the first day he started writing, and several of his novels are banned in his home country. But what really gets him into trouble are the comments and speeches he gives on current affairs.

Since the summer of 2018, Chen has been banned from posting anything on his Weibo microblog account, and he is not allowed to appear in any public event in Fujian province, where he lives and works. This was after he publicly criticised the Chinese government and the ruling Communist Party for a kindergarten scandal the previous winter, when parents said toddlers were drugged and injected with unknown substances at a nursery in Beijing.

The authority had long talks with Chen and tried to push him to "make up the mistakes" by writing some books with "positive energy".

"I think, as a writer, I would rather stop writing than write something I don't believe in," Chen told Index. "If you use your words to glorify and brag about something that doesn't deserve it, only because you are afraid of offending the power, then you are not a writer but a liar."

If you use your words to glorify and brag about something that doesn't deserve it, only because you are afraid of offending the power, then you are not a writer but a liar

CREDIT: (author) Chen Xiwo; (illustration) Rebecca Hendin

Chen is pessimistic about freedom of speech in China. "I remember when the Cultural Revolution was ended, we thought we would never have another culture revolution, but today it looks like maybe we were wrong," he said. "After the 1989 Tiananmen [Square] protest, I believed China would have to change its [political system], but it didn't and it gets more powerful and strong, based on the old authoritarian ruling."

Although family relationships are always complex, cruel and sometimes twisted in his stories, Chen says his family is his most important support. "I never told my parents about the problems I face from writing critical words," he said. "They are old and I don't want them to share the pressure. I will be even more true to myself after my parents pass away – when I have nothing to be afraid of from being sharp and critical." ⊛

Karoline Kan is a Beijing-based journalist and author of Under Red Skies, an autobiography

Vita

"LOOK, IT'S LIKE a worm!" She rolled down her waistband and showed her belly to my mum.

She was always like that, took no notice of whether I was there or not. She probably figured I was just a child. But I was eight years old, big enough to use the men's toilet.

She was our neighbour. She worked as a teacher in the local primary school and sometimes I wondered if she showed her belly like that in the school. She probably couldn't help it, her belly was proof of how she'd suffered. White worm-like things really did crawl over it, they were horrible. Much later, I learned they were called stretch marks.

"They've never faded," she complained, rubbing her hands over them. "It's been eight years! They've gone a bit lighter, but now they're white and they look worse than ever!"

The most conspicuous mark on her belly was the surgery scar, which reared upwards, hideous. I didn't know it was from a Caesarean. My mum didn't have one of those, only wrinkles on her belly. If I touched them, my mum used to tell me I'd done something bad to her.

"You were inside here," she told me, "and you pushed it out like a balloon and then you came out. That's why my belly looks like a balloon that's been blown up and then had the air let out of it. It'll never go back to how it was."

I played with balloons, so I knew what they were like when you let the air out. Imagine, I'd already given my mum a hard time before I came out of her, and then I'd left her looking worse than before. Pregnant women were ugly: waddling along with their big bellies stuck in front of them, fat, clumsy, their skin rough and freckled, brown patches on their noses. But, of course, pregnant women were loved and revered too. There was lots written in praise of women who nurtured babies and gave life to them.

Sometimes, my mum would run her fingers over our neighbour's scar.

"They cut me open, and the scar refuses to fade!" said the neighbour.

"Haven't you tried egg white?" asked my mother.

"Of course I have, I've tried everything. Restorative cream, scar tissue remedies, but nothing works! Fresh-laid eggs boiled for ages. I even got my own hen for the eggs, but that got me into trouble with the neighbourhood committee, they told me keeping a hen was unhygienic. It was because the neighbours complained so much…"

Not us, though. We didn't move in until afterwards, and we never knew she'd kept a hen. It was hard to imagine someone like her, a teacher, keeping a hen.

"When I gave birth, it hurt like hell. I thought I was passing over to the other side!" she went on.

"Passing over to the other side." She was fond of clichés like that. My mum laughed because she thought she was exaggerating. "It's true!" the woman said. "The baby was in the wrong position, she was breach. I was in agony for ages, and finally I had a Caesarean. What was the point of going through all that agony? If I'd known, I'd have had the operation at the start. But the nurses didn't want me to, they said a natural birth was better for the baby. I went through hell for Vita."

Vita – "Life" – that was what she'd called her daughter. Vita was playing nearby, making like she hadn't heard anything her mum was saying. But she must been listening in. "Little pitchers have big ears," as my mum and dad used to say if I eavesdropped. Vita was amusing herself by rubbing a corner of the table with one finger until it shone like the blade of a knife.

The neighbour often complained like this about her daughter. Sometimes she called her "blood-sucker". She said that giving birth to her had given her chronic health problems – now she couldn't stand the cold or draughts, she felt clammy, her limbs had no strength, her back ached "as if it's broken". She suffered from rheumatism, especially on dark, rainy days, and it was worse in winter. And her head ached.

"It's worse than dying! I gave my life for Vita!" she exclaimed.

Listening to her complaints, I really felt she might be better off dead. The only thing that kept her alive was her daughter. Of course she also said that it was her husband who had brought this about. "He just takes his pleasure, and it brings all this suffering on us women!"

My mum went a bit red. Why did she say it was her husband who had brought this about? I hadn't the faintest idea. But I did feel that she was being unjust to her husband. She just blamed the first person who came into her head – it didn't matter whether it was her daughter or her husband. But her daughter's sin was clear for all to see, and her daughter apparently felt the same way. She just lowered her head and accepted her guilt. Actually, she was really well-behaved, docile and obedient. My mother often said to me: "Darling, if you were only half as much like her….!"

The trouble was, the girl only had her mother, no one else to protect her. With me, if my dad laid into me, my mum would protect me. But although Vita had a father, her mother was in complete control. The gossip had it that her father had divorced her mother because he couldn't stand her temper. The mother said that her husband was stupid, but the fact was, she was only a supply teacher while the father was a university graduate. The year they got married, he passed the entrance exams. That was the year they were reinstated, after the Cultural Revolution, and university students enjoyed huge prestige. No sooner had he graduated than he got a well-paid job, but within just a few years salaries went down, just as manual labourers' wages were going up, and he became yet another impoverished intellectual. He wanted to earn some extra income on the side, but as soon as he mentioned it to his wife, she forbade it.

"No way!" She emphasised the words by wagging her finger at him the way she always did. Then she listed the reasons. Anyone who was a teacher always had plenty of reasons to justify themselves. Finally she asked: "What can you do anyway?"

She looked sideways at her husband. She never looked him straight in the eyes.

She took charge of every decision and he was resigned to it and let her do it. Whatever she said, they did. But that didn't please her either.

"You push everything onto me. Why don't you act like a husband, like a proper man?"

→ Everyone said that if they hadn't married before he went to university, he would never have married her. But he did, and he didn't do what so many men do and kick her out. He was a good man. Of course, some people said that he stayed with her because of their daughter. All the same, after one almighty row, he finally walked out and divorced her.

When the neighbours talked about the neighbour, they shook their heads. "A woman shouldn't be so dominating!" But my mum sympathised with her. Whichever way you looked at it, a woman heading up the household didn't have an easy time of it. After the divorce, she never remarried. She brought up the girl on her own, getting by on her meagre salary, and on the bit of money her ex-husband paid as child maintenance.

"I couldn't manage it if it were me," my mum said, with a coy look at my dad.

He laughed. "You won't get the chance to try!"

My mum saw a lot of the woman. They used to get together and chat. What about? Well, the ex-husband died, so they couldn't talk about husbands. They talked about children. That was what the woman really liked talking about. Actually, the two women each talked about their own, not the other's. Mothers all over the world only have their heads full of their own children.

The girl never dared cry because that would only make the blows rain down harder. She told me she didn't like piano

---

"My Baobao…" my mum would begin.

"Right, my Vita…" the woman would say.

"Right… my Baobao…"

"Right, my Vita…"

They talked about how well we kids were doing. But they criticised us too. For instance, sometimes my mum would say how naughty I was: a little devil! (But of course everyone knows that a naughty boy is a bright boy.)

The woman's daughter was altogether better-behaved. She wasn't naughty at all, she was a good girl. But "good" was simple, "good" was dull. Only naughtiness was vivid and vibrant. Having said her daughter was a good girl, there wasn't much else she could say, there was nothing to expound on, and that put her in a bad mood, so she'd up and leave. The two women often parted on bad terms, but that didn't stop them getting together for a chat on another day, and greeting each other as cheerfully as if their tiff had never happened. Being a mum was weird, it was like they couldn't live without each other, they needed each other for an audience.

But I never understood why that woman complained so much about the trials and tribulations of bringing up her daughter. Maybe it was her way of expressing her affection. Because she really did love the girl. I saw her go without food to feed her child. She would drop the food in front of her and command: "Eat up!"

The girl bowed her head and ate it up, with obvious enjoyment. And the mother would bark at her: "No one's going to take it away from you! Eat it all up, all of it!"

It seemed to give her the same satisfaction as eating the food herself. That girl was her very life, that was why she called her Vita. All the same, sometimes she'd bark "blood-sucker!" at her.

It was true that giving birth to her daughter nearly had cost her her life. And the mother blamed the girl for that. When I was older, I read up on it and understood that mother-daughter relationship properly. The woman's near-death birth experience reinforced the tight bond between the two of them. Life existed because of suffering, and the most concrete form of suffering was physical pain. Love couldn't exist without pain. When mothers talked about their children, they often talked about their bodies, something fathers wouldn't do. Men only talked about the bodies of their lovers. That was something I only realised many years later. When a man loves a woman, it's the love of a rod prodding into another body; when a woman loves her children, it's the love of a piece of flesh pulled from a body. The flesh is hers, that's why she needs to hang onto it. She feels she's on a mission. It's herself she's hanging on to. Her desires and her daughter's desires, they are one and the same. She can make those decisions. And the decision that that woman made that most astonished the neighbours was to buy her daughter a piano. I overheard her tell my mum that she was going to buy it for her daughter because when she was at school, she had wanted to play the piano but the family were too poor, so she couldn't.

"No one had that kind of money in those days!" she said. "Children nowadays are so lucky!"

In fact they were still not well-off. But she was determined to buy one and she did. The next day, the piano arrived, carried on the shoulders of six labourers, to the astonishment of all and sundry.

"It looks like they're tearing the house down!" the neighbours exclaimed.

As everyone crowded around for a better look, the woman instructed the workers. No wagging her index finger this time, she brandished both arms. They were long and thin and she waved them around, left to right, up and down. The labourers were completely bamboozled.

That evening, my mum said to my dad: "Those arms of hers, they get everyone worked up!"

My dad jokingly said: "And that piano's getting you down, is it?"

My mum wanted a piano too, but my dad said there was no hurry, a piano was a big purchase, a lot of money, and when they had the money they should think carefully how they were going to spend it. They could send me for lessons at the piano teacher's house, for instance, and only buy a piano when I'd made some progress. It was a good thing they didn't buy one because after two lessons I said I didn't want to learn piano anymore. I tried to get out of going, my mother gave me a telling-off, I cried, and there was uproar at home. Then my father spoke: "We haven't bought a piano," he said. "If he doesn't want to learn, let him be."

My dad stuck up for me, but our neighbour's daughter had no one to stick up for her. Her mother forced her to learn. She was one fierce woman, and she used to beat her daughter.

→ The girl never dared cry because that would only make the blows rain down harder. She told me she didn't like piano. Once, after a bad beating, she said fiercely that she wanted to smash the piano. Of course, she was just talking, she wouldn't have dared actually do it, or her mum would have beaten her to death. She was terrified of her mother. Once, I was talking to her and she clamped her mouth shut and her face went dead. I turned around and there was her mum standing there. She somehow sensed her, even when her mum was standing behind her. It was like she had a sixth sense.

After the piano was bought, the neighbours often heard the woman shouting and hitting her daughter in the middle of the night. It was almost always because the girl hadn't done enough piano practice. The mother would shout things like: "I've such a hard life, I'm exhausted with work and housework, I'm on my own, I'm not well!" Sometimes, she'd rant on about the father too: he never did anything to help, he was irresponsible and heartless. When she talked about her body and about not being well, she was obviously putting the blame on her daughter.

"It's all because of you that I'm like this! My life's ruined and now you're trying to kill off what's left of me! Blood-sucker, that's what you are! Heartless! Just like your dad!"

Sometimes, in the dead of night, I'd be woken from a pleasant dream by her yelling. It gave me the creeps. I snuggled down inside my quilt and thanked my lucky stars that I'd been born into my family.

"If only I'd known, I'd never have had you! Idiot girl! You're useless!" On and on she went, working herself up into a fury and finally yelling: "You're not my daughter. Get out of here! Get lost!"

I actually thought that would have been for the best. If the daughter did "get lost", she'd be out of the woman's evil clutches. We were still kids, but if she didn't leave, she might be beaten to death. At least if she went she could get a life. But would the woman really throw her daughter out? She wanted her there so she could abuse her. She beat her for the slightest thing. I felt she got pleasure out of beating her. I even felt she'd had the girl just so that she could have someone to beat.

....

*Translated by **Nicky Harman***

***Chen Xiwo** is one of China's most controversial authors. A winner of the Chinese Literature Media prize, he began publishing the short stories and novellas for which he is best-known in 2002. His story collection The Book of Sins was published in English in 2014*

On the road

Author **Helen Stevenson** introduces an exclusive translation for Index of the screenplay for Le Camion by **Marguerite Duras**, who wrote the Oscar-nominated script of Hiroshima mon Amour

48(03): 79/88 I DOI: 10.1177/0306422019874283

LEFT: French novelist, screenwriter, scenarist, playwright and film director Marguerite Duras

IT WOULD NEVER have occurred to the French writer and experimental filmmaker Marguerite Duras that she did not have the right to express herself at all times and in all circumstances exactly as her truth demanded.

Her distrust of all forms of authoritarian ideology is a constant throughout her work, influenced – as she was – by the struggles in 20th-century Europe, where countries on the continent succumbed to the violence of fascism and communism.

Her most famous screenplay, for which she received an Oscar nomination, was for the Alain Resnais film, Hiroshima Mon Amour, which she wrote out of "weariness with the cinema of consumption". She explored the erotic relationship between a Japanese man and a French nurse in Hiroshima in 1957. One of the first new wave films written at the beginning of the cold war, it cuts from the story of the couple to

pictures of the after-effects of the nuclear bomb which the Americans had dropped on the city only 12 years before. It also includes flashbacks to the main female character's memories of having a German soldier as a lover during the war. Not only was the film a lot more overtly sexual than most 1950s movies, but the theme of sleeping with the enemy and the sharp critique of the use of the nuclear bomb to end the war were taboo for many at the time. The film was pulled from the 1959 Cannes Film Festival to assuage American sensitivities.

Duras was born in the first year of World War I in French Indochina, now Vietnam the daughter of two French schoolteachers. Her father died when she was very small and her desperately impoverished mother – who always hoped her daughter would make money – bought a rice farm in a place where the land was constantly being lost to the sea.

Duras's 1984 Prix Goncourt-winning novel, L'Amant, about the 15-year-old's affair with a wealthy Chinese man, sold five million copies in four weeks and was felt to be an account of that period, even though it was not strictly true.

Duras left to study in Paris aged 18. She joined the French Communist Party and during the German occupation she worked for the Resistance, while also working for the paper supply section of the Vichy government. A year before her husband, Robert Antelme, was deported to the concentration camp at Buchenwald, she published her first novel, Les Impudents. From then on, the horror of the death camps informed everything she ever thought, felt and expressed.

Although she remained a member of the Communist Party for seven years, she suffered from its restrictive and patriarchal structure and claimed that she became truly *de gauche* only once she left, and learned "to despise no one" – though she spoke out bitterly against the Soviet Union, saying: "The century's greatest hope has become its greatest failure."

As she built a career as one of the greatest of French writers she was always of the moment, both universal and timely.

For her, 1968 was *jouissif*, a joyful explosion of revolutionary feeling. Politics were spiritual: "It's all as if God did exist." But she lost faith in politics, as one might lose faith in God. Love, alcohol and writing filled the void left by both. She had no wish to live in the 21st century, in which "all conditions were

She had no wish to live in the 21st century, in which 'all conditions were present for the experience of the utmost ennui, the futile expectation that something might happen...'

CREDIT: Sipa/Shutterstock

→ present for the experience of the utmost *ennui*, the futile expectation that something might happen…"

The Lorry (Le Camion), an extract of which is published in English for the first time below, is scarcely a story, more a proposition containing all other possible stories.

The script is cast in the conditional mood, the tense children use when they propose a make-believe game which is also deadly serious. Duras

BELOW: Still from the film Le Camion which was first released in 1977 featuring Gerard Depardieu and Marguerite Duras

sits reading the script with French actor Gerard Depardieu in a dark room (a metaphor for a photographic darkroom in which characters not seen on screen are imagined). On a road in northern France, she tells us, not far from the sea, a woman hitches a ride in a lorry and speaks to the driver about love, politics, life, anti-semitism, the "massacre of the earth".

Perhaps she does the same thing every night, her way of making the world more tolerable. Occasionally the camera cuts to the lorry, travelling, or the road the two travellers see ahead. The music is Beethoven:

the Diabelli variations.

All through her life, Duras affirmed the limitless potential of the text. The sea, the mother, the wind, love, loneliness – these are the words she puts on the page, which contain the possibility of, and carry, all other words. "I don't always quite understand what I'm saying, but I know it's true." ⊗

Helen Stevenson is a translator and the author of Instructions for Visitors and a memoir, Love Like Salt

CREDIT: Auditel/Kobal/Shutterstock

The Lorry

DARKROOM

GERARD DEPARDIEU What is she doing waiting in the road?

MARGUERITE DURAS Several explanations would have been possible. She could have gone from one place to another for personal reasons; for example, her car's broken down and she needs to rejoin her family, the place is deserted, she stops the first passing car...

(Beat.)

G.D. Or?

M.D. Nothing. Nothing to do.

(Beat.)

She is travelling around.

Silence.

G.D. When she climbs into the lorry is the main goal therefore reached?

M.D. Yes. Given the fact that they are enclosed in the same place for a certain time, locked up, you see, locked up in the same place for a certain time, that's the main point. They see the same landscape. At the same time. From the same space.

(Beat.)

The difference between them would have been the very subject of the film. And their confinement inside the lorry's cab, the first space.

Silence.

G.D. Between her and him... the driver and the lady...?

What?

What would have happened?

M.D. She would have spoken from time to time during the trip, you see.

Of the countryside. Of the wind. Of recent scientific discoveries. Of how difficult transportation is in that region.

Of a child called Abraham.

Of love.

She would have said suddenly:

There is no story outside of love.

G.D. Did anyone ask her anything?

M.D. No, but you see, she would have been somewhat incoherent, making her points in a rambling way.

G.D. It would have been a film about... love?

M.D. Yes. About everything.

It would have been a film about everything.

→ About everything at the same time:

About love.

> SIDE ROAD. *Wheat fields.*
>
> *No text.*
>
> *In the distance, the lorry is seen. It crosses the screen.*
>
> *Music.*
>
> DARKROOM

M.D. I see them shut up in the cab, as if threatened by the outside light.

> *(Beat.)*

I feel as though you and I, too, are threatened by the same light that they are frightened of: the fear that all of a sudden the lorry's cab, this darkroom, may be flooded by a stream of light, you see…

The fear of a catastrophe: Political intelligence.

> *Silence.*

G.D. An activist is someone who has no doubts.

M.D. That's it.

Inspired by specific demands that are supposed to better his lot, all of a material nature.

G.D. Material…

M.D. Yes… better housing… easier transportation… cheaper holidays: that's the main goal of his struggle.

G.D. Would he have spoken about it?

M.D. The driver? No. He would have thought that it was not worth talking about.

She would have spoken all alone almost all the time.

G.D. Does he see her?

M.D. No. He sees nothing.

He is caught between two affiliations.

He only sees things in relation to them.

I forgot to tell you that she would have been subjected to that omnipotence, the rule by a class which decides the fate of all the other classes.

When she was young.

And then also after.

G.D. Would their alienation have been equal?

M.D. Yes, because of this it would have been equal.

> *Silence.*

M.D. The last avatar of the supreme Saviour, the proletariat.

She'd believed it.

A sacred God: the proletariat.

She'd believed it.

No one has the right to question the proletariat's responsibility.

She'd believed it.

The responsibility of the activist should never be called into question again – that would mean risking blasphemy against the working class.

She'd believed it.

No one dared, no one dares anymore to call into question the responsibility of the working class: blasphemy.

She hadn't dared.

For a long time.

> *Silence.*

M.D. And then one day she saw:

The complicity between the owners and the workers.

Their identical fear.

Their identical goal.

Their identical politics: the infinite delay of any free revolution.

Killing the other man in each man, robbing him of his fundamental nature: his own contradiction.

> *Silence.*

And then one day, she saw.

It was summer.

The clowns, on the tanks, entering Prague.

> *(Beat.)*

Maybe you remember?

These paint-faced, smiling, gently brainless men.

These new killers.

This result obtained through the clash between capitalism and socialism.

A result they were proud of.

> *(Beat.)*

For a long time she watched without seeing.

And then, that day, she saw.

> *Silence.*

G.D. There is only one type of anxiety: material.

The anxiety belongs to the working-class.

Only this material anxiety is worth taking into account.

The anxiety of the others?

M.D. That of the others, nothing:

Class privilege.

> *Silence.*

Listen. She's singing.

She closes her eyes and sings.

Then, he says: I get it. You've escaped
from the psychiatric asylum of Gouchy

CREDIT: Keystone-France/Getty

→ *FOREST. Pan shot.*

In the foreground, frozen puddles. Behind, a birch tree forest white with frost.

Music.

At the end of the pan shot, a road. The lorry. It drives along the forest, crosses the
screen, very slowly.

VOICE-OVER M.D. You can hear the sea.

Far away.

Loud.

    (Beat.)

And then she would have spoken of other towns.

Of many other towns.

Less far away.

Between the vineyards ... caught between vineyards and rivers.

Other rivers.

She would have said she remembered them less precisely.

He doesn't ask which ones.

(Beat.)

She sings.

She closes her eyes.

Sings.

DARKROOM

M.D. She speaks: she tells the driver: You are from the French Communist Party.

G.D. He tells her: that's none of your business.

M.D. That's it.

She tells him: you know, Karl Marx, that's all over.

She always says the first names: Marcel Proust. Pierre Corneille. Leon Trotsky. Karl Marx...

...some kind of obsession...

Silence.

G.D. He is looking at her...

M.D.

(Beat.)

Yes...it's true.

G.D. For the first time.

M.D. So it would seem so, yes.

G.D. What is he thinking? What is he saying?

M.D. He says: I get it.

You are a reactionary.

G.D. What is her answer?

M.D. Nothing. She laughs.

(Smiles. Silence.)

M.D. Then, he says: I get it. You've escaped from the psychiatric asylum of Gouchy.

→ *(She reads.)*

That's it, Gou-chy.

(Beat.)

G.D. She doesn't understand?

M.D. Yes, yes. She answers:

(Smile.)

Do you know it?...

Did you see, they've enlarged the buildings along the river, southside, where it slopes down.

That's good... On the north side, it all opens onto the forest...

It was necessary to do it. It had become too small lately...

Silence.

G.D. He asks:

Are you involved in politics?

M.D. That's it...That's it.

She answers:

No. Not involved.

I'm not involved in anything.

I've never been involved in anything.

SIDE ROAD, the region of Chavenay (Yvelines).

Wheat fields. No text. The lorry appears in the distance, disappears, descends. Crosses
the screen.

Music (Diabelli's theme).

DARKROOM

M.D. She could also go to see her daughter

Who has just given birth.

Silence.

She says:

Imagine, my daughter has just given birth and my car broke down the very day I had to leave.

(Beat.)

It's a boy.

The birth wasn't too bad.

(Beat.)

Since my nephew, that day, had to meet his brother, who lives where my daughter lives, I told myself that I could leave with him, but we missed each other by an hour, so it didn't work out. Then what? I took the train to meet my sister right away without telling her in advance and, of course, when I arrived, there was no one, no one: a neighbour told me that my sister had gone to see a friend and wouldn't be back till the evening.

So I decided to stop the first passing car.

(Beat.)

My sister lives in the middle of nowhere. There is only one train a day and it comes at impossible hours.

(Beat.)

I did try to call her, but the operators told me that the local phone lines were down because of a storm.

That happens often in the coastal areas.

The wind. The wind, you see.

It's a huge plateau. Nothing stops the wind. Nothing, not a tree. It's barren.

The trees are uprooted by the wind – or twisted, laid down as if massacred.

(Beat.)

She sings.

A long silence. While "she is singing", M.D. places the manuscript on the table.

M.D.

(takes back the manuscript)

She's stopped singing.

(Beat.)

She says: Excuse me, I sing because I'm happy because of this child, you see, please forgive me.

I must also tell you that I'm always somewhat confused. I've never been able to put my ideas in order, to follow an idea without noticing another on its way.

Oh, just don't listen to me, in the end, that's what they say in my circle: don't mind her.

Listen, it's not all the time; I sometimes say more sensible things – more serious things, as they say.

(Beat.)

I also sometimes go silent for a long time… yes…

(Beat.)

To tell the truth, it creeps up on me like on everyone else: speaking, going silent. Being sad, or full of joy.

(Beat.)

But this, without any rules, it seems, it's what they don't like in my circle, this mental disturbance, but you see… after all, I could reply that the fact that I don't grasp a given logic doesn't mean that I don't have some kind of logic of my own. They call me too self-centred. You must have heard the word. It's used often. In principle, it's offensive. It's something one says of children. Too self-centred, he is too self-centred, she is too self-centred.

Silence.

I think the child is called Abraham. I hope this won't be difficult for him.

(Beat.)

My daughter wanted to call him that. Her husband didn't really agree.

(Beat.)

→   He said he was afraid for the child, for its future, simply because it would bear this name.

(Beat.)

She insisted. Her husband said they had to forget all those names, those Jewish words. He said that naming a child Abraham encouraged the worst collective psychosis, all the discriminations and pogroms.

My daughter didn't budge; she called her child Abraham.

Her husband is in the French Communist Party, which says it all. He was afraid they would call him a racist if he called his son Abraham. He was afraid. He said that he saw no point in calling a child such a name, a non-Jewish child.

I have to tell you that we are not Jews – no. Or Arabs.

Neither Jews nor Arabs.

(Beat.)

My daughter thinks that poetry is the most shared thing in the world, together with love. And hunger.

(Beat.)

She always talks about a counter-knowledge that supposedly happens in us at each moment; we reject it, but in vain, she says. She says: fortunately, because otherwise we would have to wait for the death of the dead.

(Beat.)

I think she's talking about her husband.

Silence.

The birth was rather painful, but the child didn't suffer.

(Beat.)

She sings.

....

Translated by **Daniela Hurezanu** *and* **Eireene Nealand**

Marguerite Duras, *who died in 1996, is one of France's most famous authors and experimental filmmakers. Her script for the film Hiroshima Mon Amour in 1959 earned her a nomination for Best Original Screenplay at the Oscars and Le Camion competed for the Palme d'Or at the Cannes film festival in 1977*

SCIENCE
MUSEUM

10 JUL 2019–
23 FEB 2020

BOOK FREE
TICKETS NOW

FROM CIPHERS
TOP SECRET
CYBER   TO
SECURITY

EXPERT ADVISORS

GCHQ
100 years

PRINCIPAL FUNDER

Department for
Digital, Culture,
Media & Sport

PRINCIPAL SPONSORS

Raytheon   avast   DXC.technology

MAJOR SPONSOR

QINETIQ

MEDIA PARTNER

The Telegraph

Muting young voices

Liverpool Poet **Brian Patten** talks to **Lewis Jennings** about his fears over schools stifling children's creativity and introduces a new poem

48(03): 90/93 I DOI: 10.1177/0306422019874288

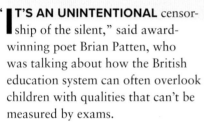

LEFT: Liverpool Poet Brian Patten

"**IT'S AN UNINTENTIONAL** censorship of the silent," said award-winning poet Brian Patten, who was talking about how the British education system can often overlook children with qualities that can't be measured by exams.

Patten's new poem, Now, Wash Your Hands, written exclusively for Index and published below, critiques how children's talents are surpressed by a rigid school curriculum which defines intelligence through exams. It also, argues Patten, crushes their creativity and ideas.

"Many teachers despair at having their hands tied by exams," said Patten, one of the three Liverpool Poets whose rebellious style made them famous in the 1960s. "They despair that no time is available to coax and nurture talents or ambitions that don't fit into preconceived notions. Exams are dictated by people whose sole idea of the purpose of education is to prepare children for Oxbridge."

Patten became a radical voice in the world of poetry, when Liverpool was the focal point of a music and arts revolution. It was led by The Beatles and took the world by storm. Patten captured this mood alongside Adrian Henri and Roger McGough in their anthology The Mersey Sound, subsequently earning the trio the freedom of the city of Liverpool in 2001.

"[We challenged] the assumption that poetry was something high-brow and for an elite," he said. "We mixed poetry and humour and treated poetry readings as theatrical performance rather than recitals. One literary critic wrote: 'They write for the great unwashed.' Another wrote that it was appalling how anyone could consider it poetry."

Fast-forward more than 50 years

Schools are now so focused on exams that those children who are 'not good' at exams – but who have emerging talent not covered by standardised assessment – are being ignored

since the best-selling anthology was first released and Patten is still writing. Featured alongside one of his latest poems, Now, Wash Your Hands which he wrote exclusively for Index, Patten has also given Index permission to publish, The Minister for Exams, which similarly focuses on the consequences of exams and the suppression of children's imagination as a result.

"I'm not saying we should leave children to splash paint around and do only what they want at school," said Patten, who is working on a new collection and memoir. "What I am saying is that schools are now so focused on exams that those children who are 'not good' at exams – but who have emerging talent not

covered by standardised assessment – are being ignored. I mean all kinds of creative children – tomorrow's craftsmen, inventors, dreamers, musicians, chefs, actors, builders, film-makers, architects… all these and more."

Patten knows how children can strive when their voices are heard and teachers allow them to nurture their talents – something he now thanks his own teachers for doing.

Having started school at the age of five, Patten was the last to learn how to read in his class. When his headmaster, Mr Wooly, once stormed into a classroom and pulled him out, he assumed he was in big trouble.

"I thought he'd found out about some misdemeanour – smoking or

fighting," Patten said.

"Instead it was because of an essay I'd written. He moved me to the A-stream where I was taught by Mr Sutcliffe. He read horror stories to the class and told us about his life at sea. He even tried to get us to like opera. A failed experiment, but when he told the story of the Flying Dutchman, doomed by the devil to sail the oceans, we were all ears. He encouraged me to write. Let me off other lessons to do so." ⊗

Lewis Jennings *is the editorial assistant at Index on Censorship*

Now, Wash Your Hands

First, take out the entire tongue.
Flatten it on a sterilised board.
Cut out the bit that asks, 'Why?'

Next, feeling along the underside you will find
The little lump that says, 'but I'd rather do…'
Dispose of this as well.

On the tip of the tongue you will discover
The place where unspoken words ferment
Cut. Add to the pile.

Sew the child's tongue back in.
Now, wash your hands.
Go and wash your hands.

The Minister For Exams

When I was a child I sat an exam.
This test was so simple
There was no way I could fail.

Q1. Describe the taste of the Moon.

It tastes like Creation I wrote,
it has the flavour of starlight.

Q2. What colour is Love?

Love is the colour of the water a man
lost in the desert finds, I wrote.

Q3. Why do snowflakes melt?

I wrote, they melt because they fall
on to the warm tongue of God.

There were other questions.
They were as simple.

I described the grief of Adam
when he was expelled from Eden.
I wrote down the exact weight of an elephant's dream

Yet today, many years later,
For my living I sweep the streets
or clean out the toilets of the fat hotels.

Why? Because constantly I failed my exams.

Why? Well, let me set a test.

Q1. How large is a child's
imagination?

Q2. How shallow is the soul of the
Minister for Exams?

....

Brian Patten is one of the Liverpool Poets, who rose to
fame in the 1960s. He is currently working on a new poetry
collection

Finding poetry in trauma

Lewis Jennings interviews taboo-breaking poet **Dean Atta** about his new poem, which deals with male rape

LEFT: Poet Dean Atta

48(03): 94/97 | DOI: 10.1177/0306422019874286

"**MEN ARE EXPECTED** to be strong, regardless of sexuality. I think physical strength is how men are thought about," said award-winning poet Dean Atta.

"Like women are expected to be emotionally strong, men are thought to be physically strong. I think the idea of being raped undermines that for some."

Atta, who was named as one of the most influential LGBT people in the UK by the Independent on Sunday Pink List of 2012, tackles male rape in his new poem, When I Was Raped, published for the first time below. Its gut-wrenching imagery feels like a voyeuristic intrusion into Atta's personal trauma – an ordeal he got to grips with while writing it.

"It would be quite difficult to write exactly how I felt when it had first happened because it was too jumbled and I had to make sense of it," he told Index. "So for me, now, I guess I've had to edit it and be a bit more forgiving to myself because it's

not my fault. No one has the right to do that. With time, people can see that more and more."

Going into the process of writing the poem, having only told his therapist and a friend about the incident, Atta knew there was the possibility it would open up a conversation with his loved ones that he was not sure he was ready to have just yet – if ever.

This presented an unusual situation for someone who, in the past, has had no problem sharing his experiences. His book I Am Nobody's Nigger offered perspectives on race, identity and sexuality and was shortlisted for the Polari First Book Prize in 2014.

"I state in this poem that the person wasn't necessarily bigger or stronger than me, but I still felt that I had been violated by them," he said. "We kind of broaden our shoulders and make ourselves bigger in situations where we feel threatened. Fight or flight, that's it for us. To freeze up

is a different response.

"We feel like we own our sexuality, but then rape almost feels like – this is just me for myself – a punishment for being a sexual being and the best way to be is to be non-sexual or only sexual within the confines of what you're told is a relationship or marriage, or something like that. But these things happen in relationships and marriages as well, so it's a false dichotomy."

When not writing award-winning poetry, Atta can be found at open mics and running workshops for schoolchildren. He also performs in drag while reading extracts from his recent novel, The Black Flamingo. The coming-of-age story, told in verse, follows a mixed-race gay teen who finds his wings as a drag artist.

Atta, who is of Greek Cypriot and Jamaican descent, is a firm believer that as long as you have a language you can make poetry.

"Whether it's written or spoken, all you need is a voice of some kind, and that requires some power and entitlement to claim that voice and use it. Once you get to that place it's yours, and that's a wonderful thing." ⊗

Lewis Jennings is the editorial assistant at Index on Censorship and the 2018 Tim Hetherington fellow

CREDIT: (top) Rosie Gilbey (right) stereotype/iStock

We kind of broaden our shoulders and make ourselves bigger in situations where we feel threatened. Fight or flight, that's it for us

When I Was Raped

I was in another country for work
And I was lonely. We had spoken briefly
On Grindr, a gay 'dating' app

I invited him to my hotel room
I knew as soon as he arrived
That I wasn't attracted to him

He didn't look like his picture
But I felt obliged
We went through the motions

That led to penetration
When he was inside of me
I just wanted it to be over

I was lying on my back
With my legs on his shoulders
But I wasn't making eye contact

He ceased his thrusting
And asked me if I was alright
And I said, No

He asked me if I wanted to stop
And I said, Yes
I thought that would be the end of it

I prepared for him to pull out
Now that my consent had been withdrawn
We were making eye contact now

He said, Just let me finish
And began pounding harder
And faster than before

I don't know if it hurt now
Because it was meant to have stopped
Or because he was making it hurt

I was hurt
That my feelings had been ignored
That my wishes had been disregarded

I didn't think, I'm being raped now
I just thought, How fucking dare he?
I pushed him off and out of me

I leapt off the bed and away from him
To stand by the window across the room
He lay on my bed

He asked me to come back
And suck his dick instead
I said, No, you need to go

He asked me to help him finish
I said, No. My back was against the window
He proceeded to masturbate

He ejaculated
He got up and used the en suite bathroom
Returned and got dressed

All the time I just stood with my back against the window
Saying nothing
But thinking, How dare he? How fucking dare he?

When he left I took a screenshot of his Grindr profile
And then deleted my account
He was the fourth guy I'd hooked up with on this trip

I thought to myself, You silly slut
If you're gonna sleep around, you're bound
To encounter guys like this eventually

I thought to myself, It could've been much worse,
He could've been bigger and stronger
And forced you to continue

I thought to myself, It wasn't that bad
You're alright
I wasn't alright. I was blaming myself

I've never felt I was able to say, I was raped
Because I invited him to my hotel room to have sex
Because I didn't say No when he first penetrated me

Because I didn't say I wanted him to stop until he asked me
Because I didn't feel physically intimidated by him
But it was rape

I withdrew my consent
And he continued fucking me. For a few seconds
Without my consent. It was rape.

....

*Dean Atta lives in London. I Am Nobody's Nigger was his
debut poetry collection. His new novel The Black Flamingo
was published in August 2019*

Tales of the unexpected

A new media monitoring project and outrageous folk tales in the forest were just two of the things happening this quarter. **Sally Gimson** and **Lewis Jennings** catch up on our activities around the world

48(03): 98/100 | DOI: 10.1177/0306422019874289

ABOVE: Jeff Wasserstrom speaking about the Tiananmen Square massacre 30 years on at King's College, London

BELOW: A slideshow illustrates different images of Weimar shown at Index's summer party and magazine launch at the Goethe Institute in London

"**ALGORITHMS MAKE IT** more difficult for people to form an opinion because platforms like Twitter or Facebook are designed so that you don't see both sides of the debate," said Jessica Ní Mhainín, policy research and advocacy officer, during an Index-hosted discussion. The event, involving the lawyer, writer and UN special rapporteur on freedom of opinion and expression David Kaye, and radio presenter Timandra Harkness, was called Stop, It's the Speech Police… and the discussion centred on how to govern the internet and guarantee free speech in the process.

One of Kaye's major points was one of transparency. Platforms such as Facebook and Twitter have stringent terms and conditions for users and can interpret them as they like. But there is no way to hold the companies to account, because it is hard to know what their processes are.

Without necessarily

acting as censors, those companies are determining the boundaries of what we see online, Kaye told the audience.

Kaye said the danger was that companies could be leaned on to remove content that governments did not like, without being accountable.

Under repressive regimes, US companies might well be more liberal than the state, he said, but no platform was truly neutral and the companies that run them have entrenched interests, which can be murky.

There was more discussion about how technology and free speech interact at the Orgcon19 conference in London, run by the Open Rights group. Index was an exhibitor and our head of content, Sean Gallagher, gave a flash talk on freedom of expression. "I spoke about how you cannot get a more equal society by putting restrictions on what people can or cannot say," he said.

Workshops at Orgcon looked at subjects ranging from how companies were using people's shopping habits to predict voting behaviour to unregulated facial recognition technology. London's Metropolitan Police came under fire from Big Brother Watch for its use of facial technology on a "trial basis" without government oversight.

The chairman of the Metropolitan Police staff association Ken Marsh recently said that he thought China's use of facial recognition was "spot on" and "absolutely correct", prompting fears from human rights defenders.

Another conference Index was involved in was run by the UK Foreign Office. The Global Conference for Media Freedom was held in July and brought together organisations from around the world. Ahead of the conference Index CEO Jodie Ginsberg criticised the organisers' decision not to allow RT and Sputnik TV to attend. She said they should not be "cherry picking" which media outlets were allowed to come and added: "[Index is] extremely

CREDIT: (left and above right) Rosie Gilbey (above left and right) Sean Gallagher

You cannot get a more equal society by putting restrictions on what people can or cannot say

concerned about the message this decision sends about the UK's genuine commitment to a free and independent media worldwide."

Ginsberg chaired a panel at the conference called Taking A Stand, How We Defend Media Freedom Around the World, and Index was a main exhibitor. And Index's 2019 Freedom of Expression Journalism Award winner, Mimi Mefo, spoke about her experience working in Cameroon, where she has been persecuted for her news reporting. She told the audience how she had been jailed and said how important it was that the outside world knew about journalists' imprisonment because it helped get them released.

Past fellows also attended, including Honduran journalist Wendy Funes; internet freedom mappers Netblocks; Al Jazeera journalist and former Maldives Independent editor Zaheena Rasheed; Saudi Arabian journalist and filmmaker Safa Al Ahmad; and Syrian journalist Zaina Erhaim.

Index fellowships and advocacy officer Perla Hinojosa said: "It was wonderful that many of our fellows from around the world were able to come to the conference and it was great to see how their work was of significance to media freedom in the countries where they operate. They are brave advocates

for media freedom and many of them face threats, harassment and intimidation for their work."

Index runs programmes for its annual fellows to help them operate more safely and to address freedom of expression issues. It offers help with digital security, physical protection and advice on how to get round internet blockages, for instance. Index also helps them create networks around the world with other campaigners, artists and journalists under threat.

Hinojosa added: "We had another two fellows, Zaina [Erhaim] and Zaheena [Rasheed], and they also spoke about their issues on the ground and how that affected them: how sometimes not getting access to training is really bad; how organisations take too long to act; the importance of solidarity between the international community; and ensuring that journalists are not forgotten, even in countries that are not always high profile."

Index on Censorship's summer magazine launch was held at the Goethe Institute in London. German crime author and the chair of German Pen Regula Venske flew over from Hamburg to talk on the 100th anniversary of Weimar Republic. She told the many friends of Index who attended about the various meanings of Weimar to Germans. Weimar is remembered variously in Germany as the home of classical authors Wolfgang von Goethe and Friedrich Schiller; a period of failed democracy and economic collapse which led to Nazism; and the site of a concentration camp Buchenwald.

Chinese experts also remembered 30 years since the Tiananmen Square at a panel discussion run by Index at King's College, London. Jeff Wasserstrom, professor of history at the University of California, and Tania Branigan, foreign leader writer for The Guardian and →

ABOVE: German crime writer and chair of German Pen Regula Venske speaking about what Weimar means to Germans at Index's magazine launch and summer party at the Goethe Institute in London

LEFT: Radio presenter Timandra Harkness who talked with UN special rapporteur on freedom of opinion and expression David Kaye at an event hosted by Index about how to govern the internet and guarantee free speech

ABOVE: Performance artist Jemima Foxtrot at Index's Forest Folktales at Latitude Festival in Suffolk, England

BELOW: Previous Index Freedom of Expression award fellows Zaheena Rasheed (left) and Wendy Funes (right), at the Global Conference for Media Freedom in London

BOTTOM: Funes and Rasheed with Terry Anderson, deputy director of 2019 Index award winner Cartoon Rights Network International, and Alp Toker of NetBlocks

→ its former China correspondent, talked about the silence around the massacre in China today. Not only does the state censor public discussion about it, but there is silence in families where parents will not tell their children about their experiences then.

One of Index's new projects, which has been running since the beginning of 2019, involves mapping attacks on journalists in Russia, Ukraine, Azerbaijan, Turkey and Belarus. This is at the heart of our Monitoring and Advocating for Media Freedom Project.

Between February and April 2019 Index mapped 116 incidents across the five countries, ranging from newspaper offices being raided to physical attacks on journalists. So far in 2019 we have tracked rises in the number of fines journalists have faced, the intimidation to which they have been subjected and physical violence. Tensions are particularly marked in Russia, where newspaper offices have been ransacked and raided by the police, computers and hard drives have been destroyed and newspapers have been put out of businesses for days at a time. Sometimes this takes the form of a traditional police raid, as in the case of the local Pskov newspaper, Pskovskaya Gubernia, where a newspaper hard drive was confiscated by the police. In other cases, newspapers have found their offices destroyed by vandals who have left threats and destroyed hard drives.

The Russian government has also recently passed laws that criminalise spreading "fake news" and ban online shows of "disrespect" against the government, its officials, society and state symbols. In Azerbaijan, where media freedom is so restricted that many reporters self-censor, journalists frequently face detention and travel bans, and are often blocked from covering events.

The physical attacks on journalists have been so severe in Russia and Ukraine that Index has published a special report on the subject.

Index research manager Kira Tverskaya said: "The 20 June death of journalist and blogger Vadim Komarov, after he was attacked with a hammer in the centre of Cherkasy on 4 May, is a severe and frightening example of the violence."

In March, Index on Censorship deputy editor Sally Gimson went to the WAN-IFRA (the World Association of Newspapers and News Publishers) congress in Glasgow.

"Much of the discussion was about how newspapers are going to be funded in the future and how they are adapting. Some are developing TV stations to go with their print editions, others are experimenting with podcasts and 'voice' technology," she said. "It was generally felt that funding for infrastructure was more important than funding for individual investigative projects."

The summer finished with a flurry of activity, with Index out and about at Latitude festival in Suffolk and the Cambridge Folk Festival. Here we launched a new project, Forbidden Folktales: Uncensored.

Index head of events Helen Galliano said: "Bringing uncensored folktales to the forests of Latitude this summer was an incredible experience. We were joined by some brilliant writers including Scarlett Curtis, Max Porter and Jade Cuttle, who brought a subversive spin to well-known fairytales, including extracts from Angela Carter's gory collection of short stories The Bloody Chamber. At Cambridge Folk Festival, people joined in and brought their own uncensored versions of folktales to share at dusk in the flower tent." ⊗

*Sally Gimson is the deputy editor at Index on Censorship, and **Lewis Jennings** is the editorial assistant*

CREDIT: (below and bottom) Sean Gallagher and (above) Helen Galliano

Macho politics drive academic closures

As academics teaching gender studies around the world lose their jobs and research grants, **Sally Gimson** reports on why this is happening

48(03): 101/104 I DOI: 10.1177/0306422019874290

MARCIA TIBURI WAS a feminist professor of philosophy in Brazil. For several years she has faced death threats and serious intimidation, and she claims she was sacked from her job at Mackenzie Presbytarian University in Sao Paulo, because she advocated at a federal state event for abortion rights.

She also ran unsuccessfully for election as governor of Rio de Janeiro, during which she received 200 death threats and had to travel in a bulletproof car.

She has now fled and lives in Paris. The death threats meant that Tiburi, who is also a prize-winning author, felt she could not live safely in Brazil anymore. Her books – including the anthology Women and Philosophy and the book How to Talk to Fascists – have made her the target of abuse, ratcheted up by the anti-feminist rhetoric of the government which has seen other academics hounded out of their jobs - and the country.

"Gender is a demonised word in Brazil," she told Index. "This word has been denied, forbidden in all government documents since 2016… but Brazil was not as crazy as it has become under the government of [President Jair] Bolsonaro. I am now leaving the country because of the persecution and the threats."

Tiburi is a public academic in Brazil, but she is one of many around the world who teach gender studies, or use feminist theory in their field of study, who are finding themselves under threat in countries where a new generation of "strong" male leaders want to enforce a new set of rules. These leaders want to promote traditional conservative views of women as having their main focus on the home and children, and to fight against progressive ideas of identity and sexuality. Mackenzie Presbytarian University has been approached for a comment.

Academics are finding their programmes abolished, are coming under personal attack on social media, and are struggling for funding. Those not falling in line with these conservative ideas are often labelled as "unpatriotic" and "unscientific", interested only in peddling what has been dubbed a leftist, or even Marxist, "gender ideology".

Linda Marie Rustad, the director of Kilden, a knowledge centre for gender perspectives and gender balance in research in Norway, told Index: "This is about an attack on academic freedom. These right-wing parliaments and governments disagree on a lot, but where there is consensus is on gender." →

RIGHT: Andrea Pető, professor in the department of gender studies at Central European University, Hungary

CREDIT: Robert Haas

Rustad says that, in practical terms, research about gender and women is important and that if research is closed down, there will be less knowledge and data about women's lives and what is happening to them in society.

She adds that the global attack on gender studies is part of a wider attack on women's rights, including abortion and reproductive rights.

"What is so special about the gender field is that it's related to the women's rights movement," she said. "And what we see today is that the pressure against women is increasing."

Roman Kuhar, editor of the book Anti-Gender Campaigns in Europe, is a professor of sociology and dean of the arts faculty at the University of Ljubljana in Slovenia. He believes that populists and far-right parties tell voters that there is "a hidden plan behind the gender agenda to delete the difference between masculinity and femininity". And the issue is complicated by the fact that in many countries there are not separate words for sex and gender.

He says the attack on what was termed "gender ideology" is, for leaders ranging from Bolsonaro to Hungarian Prime Minister Viktor

CREDIT: Gary Waters/Ikon

Orbán, an easy way to unite disparate groups of people but ultimately meaningless.

It can be used to unite conservative or religious people, people who are worried about sex education in schools or who are against LGBTQ+ rights, including equal marriage, and women's reproductive rights. "It can be filled in with different meanings, and that was the trick," he told Index.

The anti "gender ideology" movement has been so successful that it is now being used in a "copy and paste" way around the world, he said.

In his inauguration speech on 1 January 2019, Bolsonaro was clear about his hatred of gender studies. He promised to "liberate" Brazil from "gender ideology", "political correctness", and "ideology that defends bandits". He has also said he wants to limit the teaching of philosophy and sociology in favour of practical studies such as engineering and medicine.

In rhetoric similar to that in Brazil, the Hungarian deputy prime minister, Zsolt Semjen, was reported by international news agency AFP as saying gender studies "has no business in universities" because it is "an ideology, not a science". And Orbán's government has withdrawn accreditation and funding for the two gender studies masters programmes in the country.

One was taught at the state-run university, Eötvös Loránd University (ELTE), and the other at the Central European University, both of which are among the top universities in Hungary. The private CEU is now moving to Vienna after a long running-battle with the government.

Andrea Pető, a professor at the CEU, is one of the victims of this ban. Her works on gender, politics, the Holocaust and war have been translated into 19 languages. And in 2018 she was awarded the All European Academies Madame de Staël Prize for Cultural Values.

She told Index she had received an anonymous threatening email via the academic website academia.edu because of what she teaches. It was also anti-semitic, saying that it "foresaw the eradication of her breed". The CEU offered to provide her with a bodyguard – an offer she turned down. Now she and other academics are fighting back.

Now, due to the campaign, Hungary – the country of 10 million – became the country of 10 million gender experts and everybody has an opinion about the reading list, learning outcome or the labour market position

Last November there were strikes at the major universities of Corvinus, ELTE and the CEU. And, says Pető, there is an open debate in the country about the issues.

"Previously, scholars of gender studies were working either in their offices, in the attic or in the cellar, but definitely marginalised," she said. "Now, due to the campaign, Hungary – the country of 10 million – became the country of 10 million gender experts and everybody has an opinion about the reading list, learning outcome or the labour market position."

And she adds that, in protest, many colleagues who were previously silent include the issue of gender on the courses they teach and quote female scholars. Gender has become "cool, a forbidden critical tool to understand our society". She says that, as a result of the current debate, her book on sexual violence during World War II in Hungary moved on to the bestseller list there for weeks.

However, the pressure is building on academic freedom in Hungary. In July, the government passed legislation which would see Orbán's government take control of the research institutes which are overseen by the Hungarian Academy of Sciences (Index 47.3, p46). Pető says that, so far, no pro-government academics have agreed to lead the process, but what happens will be a real test of academic freedom. She also says that one of the crucial factors will be whether foreign academics and research institutions will co-operate with, and legitimise, this new arrangement – one which, she points out, will be well-funded by the government.

In Poland, the squeeze on academic →

Gender is a demonised word in Brazil. This word has been denied, forbidden in all government documents since 2016

→ study of feminist and gender theory is more subtle than in Hungary and more linked to the Catholic church, according to academics. It has affected funding of academic studies, and the posts of researchers who have been accused of challenging the traditional role of the family, but it has not been put into law in quite the same way as in Hungary. For instance, the current minister of science and higher education, Jarosław Gowin, said that he wanted to withdraw funding for journals of lesbian and gay studies but has so far failed to follow through.

But female academics in the gender studies and feminist field are under pressure. In March this year the liberal arts faculty at the University of Warsaw did not renew the contract of a well-known gender studies academic and activist Ewa Majewska, who was an adjunct professor there. This sparked a protest and petition by students who called for her reinstatement.

Malgorzata Budzowska, assistant professor at the University of Lodz, in Poland, told Index that she believed Majewska had lost her job because of her area of expertise and because she had been seen as a "disloyal" researcher.

Announcing her departure on her Facebook page, Majewska wrote: "I believe that some day you will be able to be critical, [be] feminist and work calmly at the university without facing double standards, censorship, unconnected charges and ordinary exploitation."

Budzowska told Index: "In Poland the devil's name now is 'gender'. Government, hand in hand with Catholic church, abuses the idea of gender to threaten society with a leftist ideology that is supposed to destroy a traditional family."

She has also found it difficult to get funding. Her special subject is modern theatre and she publishes mostly about contemporary Polish theatre adaptations of ancient dramas. The radical theatre directors she is interested in include Maja Kleczewska, who puts on

productions of classical plays and deals with issues such as abortion and women's rights.

Budzowska has also been told by another academic that she might be unfit to teach because she is a single, divorced mother. And she worries that, were her university to elect a rector who is not as liberal and supportive as the current one, she might lose her job because of her marital status.

The attack on gender studies and related subjects is happening not just in eastern Europe and Latin America. In Germany, for instance, the far-right is taking up the agenda. As part of its manifesto, the far-right Afd party in Germany says that it would end research for gender studies, saying: "Existing university chairs for gender research should not be filled again, and ongoing gender research projects should not be prolonged."

Academics such as Kuhar believe that even in countries where there are no direct attacks on gender studies programmes, such as his native Slovenia, government ministries are still worried about giving research grants to studies on gender because of the potential political backlash.

Rustad says there needs to be more co-ordinated action by universities around the world and is worried about research grants being refused. She says international programmes which fund research should consider whether they have an ethical responsibility when they co-operate with countries where academic freedom is under threat, and that organisations which defend academic freedom should be asking themselves if a gender action plan is needed.

Kuhar is even clearer: this needs to be recognised by academics as a global problem and as a co-ordinated attack on academic freedom. ⊗

Sally Gimson *is the deputy editor of Index on Censorship*